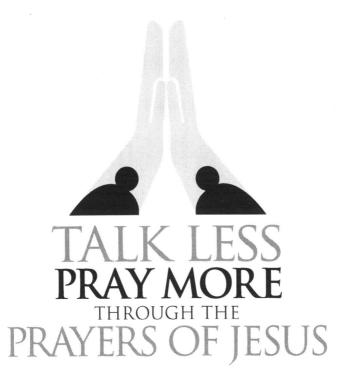

# TALK LESS
## PRAY MORE
### THROUGH THE
# PRAYERS OF JESUS

DR. GARY MILLER

Luke 11:1

# DEDICATION

This book is dedicated to my parents, Don and Libby Miller. They are the finest and the most faithful prayer warriors I know. They trained legions of prayer warriors all around the world through their Bible Based Prayer Conferences from 1976–2011. Even after retiring from the road, they continued to pray together for the next Great Awakening until my dad's passing in April 2015. The best is yet to come.

# APPRECIATION

Thank you to my wife, Dana, for her consistent encouragement to put my thoughts on prayer into this book. Thank you to my daughter, Ashley Warren, for guiding it through the editing process. Thank you to my son- in-law, Brent Warren, for his assistance with the artwork. Thank you to my daughter, Ally-son, for praying with me every morning after I finished each page. They are my treasures on Earth.

When Ashley, our first born, came into this world, it was a life-changing experience for me. I didn't know it was possible to love someone so little, so much. As I stood looking at her through the window of the maternity ward in Tulsa, Oklahoma, I heard these words from Sharon Ross. Standing next to me, she silently, and softly spoke over my shoulder, "She is a little blank slate, and you can write on her anything that you want." I was staggered by the power of my friend's simple, profound statement. I have never recovered from it. I never will. No dad ever should.

Ashley has provided immense joy to my life, and I continue to be amazed at what God has written on her heart. Her editing of this book has been an expression of her love for prayer, and for me. This book has her handprints on it, and her heartbeat in it. As a little girl, she helped me craft my storytelling skills. I have such fond memories of kneeling by her bed and telling her one of her favorites, until she fell to sleep. I am grateful to God for bestowing on me the highest calling of all, the privilege of being called Daddy, by my "Brown-eyed Girl." No title compares to it.

# CONTENTS

# INTRODUCTION

One of the earliest memories I have of my dad, Don Miller, is waking up in the mornings to see him reading his Bible in the living room and praying over his family. I can't fully explain it, but even then, before I could understand, that picture brought a peace to my heart. It still does. Until his dying day, you could find my dad, at 93 years of age, doing the same thing.

My father devoted more than half of his ministry life teaching people how to pray, and my wife, Dana, and I are honored to carry on his legacy. In 2010 we stepped out in faith from full-time pastoral ministry and founded TALK LESS! PRAY MORE!

We believe that the hope of the world is the local Church, and the strength of the Church is sustained by praying people. No program in the world can substitute for equipping people to have a passion for prayer.

This kind of believing prayer can be developed and nurtured in your personal life and in the members of your family. It just takes one person to get on their knees for the ripple effect to begin.

We recently transitioned my parents from their home of 37 years to a retirement center. But before then, one of my dad's favorite places to pray was in his "Prayer Arbor" in the back-yard. This covered swing faced east, because he was prepared to see Jesus come back. I'm honored to say that swing now sits on my front porch, and it's one of my favorite places to sit and pray.

It's why this book is in your hands.

When I began reading through Matthew, Mark, Luke, and

John, I saw a pattern of the prayers of Jesus and how they could apply to our lives today. God sent His only Son to Earth to save mankind. Jesus, both human and King, even in earthly form, cried out to His Father during his 33 years on this Earth.

I find it both reassuring and humbling that the King of kings, relied on prayer to carry Him through some of His best and darkest moments. He still does. Jesus sits at the right hand of the Father interceding for you at this very moment.

He's just waiting for you to cry out and rely on Him. Let Him carry your burdens. Allow Him the honor of entering into this new season of prayer with you. I pray this devotional guide will bring you into a deeper understanding of prayer and a hunger for intimacy with Jesus.

*Prayer is the intimate communication between the Heavenly Father and His child.* —Don Miller

# 1

# THE BAPTISM

..............................

*Now when all the people were baptized, Jesus was also baptized, and while He was praying, heaven was opened, and the Holy Spirit descended upon Him in bodily form like a dove, and a voice came out of heaven, "You are My beloved Son, in You I am well-pleased"* (Luke 3:21–22).

The Gospel of Luke records one of the earliest examples of the prayer life of Jesus. It should come as no surprise that it also documents one of the Father's earliest answers to His Son's prayer. The powerful energy and synergy of prayer is revealed within the context of these two brief verses. The Son prays, the Spirit descends, and the Father commends.

In April of 1974, I was riding out the rainy season in the Southern Highlands of Tanzania. The rainfall that month exceeded 40 inches. The roads were impassable, and work was impossible. I put on the coffee, threw a log on the fire, and I read and prayed my way through the Bible. As I read this passage of Scripture, I began to see the wisdom of praying to the Father, in the name of Jesus, and in the power of the Holy Spirit. It has served me well over the past 40 years. I encourage you to find great comfort in it.

Prayer is the catalytic converter that transforms the doctrinal concept of the Trinity into a powerful expression of the presence of God. There is simply nothing else in the world like prayer to usher in His presence. Prayer brings the Father, the Son, and the Spirit together like nothing else ever will.

*Now when all the people were baptized,*
*Jesus was also baptized* (vs. 21a).

Prayer is the essential key to any Spiritual Awakening on a personal and corporate level. Prayer thrives in the climate of obedience. Prayer expresses your spirit of dependence upon the Father. Expect Him to respond to your needs. You are His child.

As Jesus launched His public ministry, He identified with the humble spirit of repentant people who were responding to the message of John the Baptist.

While they were expressing their own public symbol of repentance, He engaged in His own private ministry of intercession.

As the sinless Son of God, Jesus had no personal need to repent of any sin. Still, His Spirit was drawn to the spirit of repentance of God's people.

Within this context of the private conviction and public repentance of God's people, Jesus was praying.

Praying led the Son to identify with the people, and yield to the symbol of baptism. It was not a symbol of His repentance of sin, but a sign of His humility and obedience to the Father. In no small measure, His heart must have been moved with compassion to identify with those whose hearts were tender to the Spirit's conviction of sin.

*And while He was praying, heaven*
*was opened* (vs. 21b).

Jesus began His ministry in prayer. Perhaps more importantly, He continues His ministry of intercession in the present tense. He is seated at the right hand of the Father. The Son lives to intercede.

*Therefore He is able also to save forever those who draw near to God through Him, since He always lives to make intercession for them* (Hebrews 7:25).

There is one glaring omission of Mel Gibson's movie, *The Passion of the Christ*. There is only a faint suggestion of the Resurrection, but no reference at all to the risen Christ's ministry of intercession.

When you wear a crucifix to honor the Savior's passion in the past tense, you would be well served to remember His intercession in the present tense.

Perhaps replacing the wearing of a crucifix with another symbol, nail-scarred, praying hands, would improve your perspective on the ministry of the living Christ.

*Christ Jesus is He who died, yes, rather who was raised, who is at the right hand of God, who also intercedes for us* (Romans 8:34).

The Bible clearly reveals, when Jesus prays, Heaven opens. This is the point of prayer. Prayer is not about sending God a "selfie." Prayer doesn't give Heaven a glimpse of your life on

Earth. Prayer brings Heaven to Earth, and makes a difference in your life. When the Son prays, the Father listens and responds with the Spirit. The intercession of God's Son provides what the Father's children need the most, His Spirit.

*The Holy Spirit descended upon Him* (vs. 22a).

The power of prayer is not a product of the tongue's eloquence, but the heart's dependence. Power is produced by the presence of the Spirit. Before the Spirit descends, believing prayers must ascend. Humbly depend on the Father as your only hope of deliverance, and yield your will to His direction, protection, and correction. Put yourself in the right position to receive the Spirit's anointing.

*Bodily form like a dove* (vs. 22b).

There is simply nothing like the presence of the Holy Spirit. There is no substitute on Earth for Heaven's gift. He is God. Not some white bird, flitting and flying around, feathering the nests of those who claim to have a permanent hold on His presence. He is the Spirit of God, and cannot be caged by you or any denomination. The dove was a sign, not a substitute. Painting a dove on the sign of a prayerless church, or wrapping a silver dove necklace around a stiff-necked, prayerless person won't bring His presence.

The Spirit can be received within the context of believing prayer, or He can be grieved by the lack of it. Humbly pray and experience His power. If you try to tap His power by dropping His name without yielding your will, you won't be touched by the power of His presence.

The Spirit is closely identified with the Son in the ministry of intercession. When the Son prayed, the Spirit descended. When the Father's children pray, the Spirit identifies with their spirit of dependence on the Father, not the eloquence of His children. The Spirit makes up for what is lacking by interpreting your choking words spewing out of your broken heart, and delivering them to the Son.

> *In the same way the Spirit also helps our weakness; for we do not know how to pray as we should, but the Spirit Himself intercedes for us with groanings too deep for words; and He who searches the hearts knows what the mind of the Spirit is, because He intercedes for the saints according to the will of God* (Romans 8:26–27).

..................................

**NOTE TO SELF:** Jesus is not on the Cross. He died. He was buried. And rose from the dead! He is seated at the right hand of the Father. He is not continually dying on a cross . . . He is praying for you. When you pray, He fills your life with His presence. PRAY!

## TALK LESS! PRAY MORE!

# 2

# THE PRIORITY

..................................

*In the early morning, while it was still dark, Jesus got up, left the house, and went away to a secluded place, and was praying there* (Mark 1:35).

Mark's Gospel reveals the habit of Jesus that undergirded the priority He placed on private, personal prayer. Before His day got away from Him, Jesus met privately with God. He undertook public ministry only after He had prayed.

One of the earliest memories of my life is seeing my father at prayer early in the morning. It didn't matter if we were at home or on vacation, his time with the Father was how he started each day. A few years ago, I asked him if he rose early to pray or if he had a sleeping disorder. He laughed and said, I have prayed and asked God to take this mantle from me and give it to you. I didn't laugh. He did. A month later, I began to awaken each morning at 4:00 a.m. Dad's prayer was answered. He always gets the last laugh.

Luke the physician and historian, served alongside Paul and Mark during the aged Apostle's first imprisonment in Rome.

Mark shared with Luke the memory of Jesus setting aside time for intimate communication with the Father before anyone or anything else could interfere with the priority of a private conversation between the Father and the Son. Luke recorded:

> *When day came, Jesus left and went to a secluded place; and the crowds were searching for Him, and came to Him and tried to keep Him from going away from them* (Luke 4:42).

The Reformer, Martin Luther, gave his best three hours to God early in the morning. Pray before your day begins and you will serve more effectively throughout your day. Prayerless intensity for the work of the Lord is a poor substitute for prayerful intimacy with the Lord of the work. Prayer warriors value intimacy over intensity.

> *Prayer is the intimate communication between the Heavenly Father and His child.* —Don Miller

Setting aside time to meet with God, early in the morning, may appear to be a forced form of communication, especially for those who aren't blessed with a biological clock that is set to rise before dawn.

The world seems to be divided among those who are morning people and those who are afflicted with morning sickness. Which one are you?

Rising early is not a major problem for me. I may not have a stronger desire for prayer—it may be a sleeping disorder. On the other hand, the snooze button was invented on purpose not by accident—people do love their sleep. The issue for Jesus was one of a private priority, not personal preference. He set one and discarded the other

Since the Father never sleeps, it is doubtful that early risers are held any closer to His heart than those who start their day a bit later. Still, Jesus started His day with the Father. Before He allowed anyone else to have a piece of Him, Jesus wanted to be at peace with His Father. People at peace with the Father are not as likely to give people who disrupt their schedule a piece of their mind.

The priority of prayer early in the day is not about the Father having time to meet with His children. It is about His children making time to meet with Him. They get with the Father before anyone else has a shot at setting the pace or suggesting a sense of direction for their day.

Perhaps the most pretentious of self-righteous people are those who have to remind those around them that they just had their "quiet time." These kinds of announcements are more irritating than inspiring.

Those who have set aside time to meet with the Father in the morning may begin this habit out of a sense of necessity, but it soon develops into intimacy. The fondness for the Father's comforting presence becomes far greater than one's own personal preference for a comforting mattress. Poet Ralph Cushman expressed it this way:

*I met God in the morning*
*When my day was at its best,*
*And His Presence came like sunrise*
*Like a glory in my breast.*
*All day long the Presence lingered,*

*All day long He stayed with me,*
*And we sailed in perfect calmness*
*O'er a very troubled sea.*
*Other ships were blown and battered,*
*Other ships were sore distressed,*
*But the winds that seemed to drive them*
*Brought to us a peace and rest.*
*Then I thought of other mornings,*
*With a keen remorse of mind,*
*When I, too, had loosed the moorings*
*With the Presence left behind.*
*So I think I know the secret,*
*Learned from many a troubled way;*
*You must seek Him in the morning*
*If you want Him through the day.*

Reformers, poets, and preachers have all discovered that there is no substitute for establishing the priority of prayer. Scottish pastor, Robert Murray M'Cheyne, who died at 29 years of age, discovered in his short life this profound truth:

*I ought to pray before seeing any one. Often*
*when I sleep long, or meet with others early,*
*it is eleven or twelve o'clock before I begin*
*secret prayer. This is a wretched system.*
*It is unscriptural. Christ arose before day*
*and went into a solitary place. David says:*
*"Early will I seek thee"; "Thou shalt early*
*hear my voice." Family prayer loses much*
*of its power and sweetness, and I can do no*
*good to those who come to seek from me.*

*The conscience feels guilty, the soul unfed, the lamp not trimmed. Then when in secret prayer the soul is often out of tune, I feel it is far better to begin with God—to see his face first, to get my soul near him before it is near another.*

Making time and having time are not mutually exclusive. The habit of the former is closely related to the availability of the latter. If you're interested in setting the priority of prayer you are going to have to discover that time of the day when it is most conducive to establish unbroken communication with the Father. It is rarely the same for everyone, and it is not likely to remain unchanged throughout your life. The point is . . . PRAY!

Setting the priority means something else will have to be interrupted or discarded to make time for prayer. Setting aside time to get with God will be rewarded. Meeting with God, before anyone else or any other interruption is worth the price you pay to set the priority.

Jesus prayed and paid it all. When you pray at all soon, you learn to do so A.S.A.P. You will gain a fresh understanding of the value of intimate communication with the Father.

...............................

**NOTE TO SELF:** If you have just spent time in the presence of God, you shouldn't have to announce it. If people can't tell it, by the look on your face, don't get in their faces and tell them about it. Jesus was thinking of you when He said, *"Beware of practicing your righteousness before men"* (Matthew 6:1).

## TALK LESS! PRAY MORE!

# 3

# THE WILDERNESS

..............................

*But the news about Him was spreading even farther, and large crowds were gathering to hear Him and to be healed of their sicknesses. But Jesus Himself would often slip away to the wilderness and pray* (Luke 5:15–16).

The scene depicted in this passage of Scripture is nothing less than a dream come true for most preachers. With everything going right all around Him, Jesus got up and left town.

When Jesus left for the wilderness, it was no fit of encore anxiety. It was His personal habit and deeply ingrained in His character. Withdrawing to the wilderness was a clear reflection of His dependence upon private intimacy with the Father. Jesus valued intimacy with the Father over the intensity of public ministry.

*But Jesus Himself would often slip away*
*to the wilderness and pray* (vs. 16).

Jesus made a habit of slipping away to pray. Those who fail to follow His lead will fail to deal with the temptation of celebrity. They soon slip up and stray. His followers, but especially His preachers, should follow His lead and get away to pray before they slip up and stray.

Public ministry sometimes leads you into the spotlight and blinds you to the danger of stepping too close to the flame of the footlights. When you don't make time to pray, you are drawn towards the light like a moth to a flame. Mesmerized by the siren sound of your own voice, you will head toward the rocks. This only happens . . . EVERY TIME.

There is genuine danger in spending too much time on the stage and too little time in the wilderness. Enjoying the sound of your own voice, and walking into your own afterglow, leads to a fall. The wise will follow Jesus and withdraw from the crowd. The wilderness provides the climate where weary followers can listen to the Father's voice to receive His fresh direction, protection, and correction.

I recall having lunch with a famous pastor who was in transition. He had resigned a prestigious pastorate and taken a sales position to provide for his family. I asked him what caused him to make such a drastic change in his life.

His response remains one of the more prophetic statements I have ever heard. The following quote is a summary of his remarks and a faithful tribute to him and his journey:

*There was a time when there wasn't a banquet, barn raising, or barbecue in this state that wasn't complete unless I was on the program. I began to enjoy hearing my own introductions, and reading my press clippings. The more I was on stage, the more blinded I was by*

*the seductive light of celebrity. Eventually, I fell off*
*the stage and found myself in the orchestra pit.*

It pleases me to say that this preacher has been restored to active and effective service. His journey has been painful to watch and it must have been excruciating to live. God's grace really is amazing.

**WHO NEEDS THE WILDERNESS?** Every Christ follower must continue walking with Jesus. He has never rescinded His first call, *"Follow Me"* (Matthew 4:19). Jesus often went to the wilderness. The wise go wild, not mild. Get with Jesus.

**WHAT IS THE WILDERNESS?** It is separated space away from others, where there is enough solitude to offer enough silence to hear from God, not others.

**WHERE IS THE WILDERNESS?** It may be a distant place, but it can be as close as a chair, a closet, or a corner of a table in a coffee shop. It may be a place or even a certain time of day.

**WHEN DO I GO TO THE WILDERNESS?** OFTEN. The word used for "often slip away" (vs. 16) communicates a spirit of compliance and a willingness to let go of what God has provided. Those who have success in ministry will not try to hold onto it with a white-knuckled grip. Those who experience failure will not consider it a permanent condition. Anytime success or failure interferes with personal intimacy with the Father, it is a time of crisis. Both conditions offer an opportunity to go to the wilderness.

You must hear from the Father, as well as gifted commentators. Downloading sermon notes from the guru of the week may provide something to say on Sunday, but only spending time alone with the Father will anoint you with a fresh word from God.

In the wilderness prayer warriors are, *deprived of the aid and protection of others, especially of friends, acquaintances, and kindred* (Blue Letter Bible Commentary). There is no easy road to the wilderness. Obstacles and excuses block the way to the flow of milk and honey. Go there anyway.

...............................

**NOTE TO SELF:** How can you get to the wilderness? This is a question each person must answer on an individual basis. At the very least, it requires the shifting of priorities, and the carving of time out of schedules already tightly packed with what appears to be very urgent matters. Seasons of life change, how you get to the wilderness may change, but the discernment between the urgent and the important is found in the wilderness.

Prayer matters because intimacy mattered to Jesus. He chose what was important over what was urgent, and found a time and a place to get alone with His Father in the wilderness. Follow Jesus and you will often get away with the Father in the wilderness.

## TALK LESS! PRAY MORE!

# 4

# THE MOUNTAIN

..............................

*It was at this time that He went off to the mountain to pray,*
*and He spent the whole night in prayer to God* (Luke 6:12).

Pulling an "all-nighter" is college talk for cramming for an exam. Jamming information into an empty head in a short period of time may not be studying, but it beats failing. Been there done that.

Praying all night is seldom turned to with the same consistency as worrying all night, fishing all night, driving all night, or a host of other things that people are willing to perform without sleep. Jesus chose praying all night to deal with His enemies and to intercede for His friends. You would be well served to follow His lead.

Luke's Gospel records more about the prayer life of Jesus than any other writer in the New Testament. Though he was not an eyewitness to the earthly ministry of Jesus, and never privileged to hear Him pray in person, the prayer life of Jesus had a powerful impact on Luke's life.

Within the context of a crisis, Jesus always turned to prayer. "It was at this time," (vs. 12). Jesus was squeezed between the rage of His enemies and the selection of His disciples.

When the Pharisees saw Jesus heal a man's withered hand on the Sabbath, they simultaneously lost their minds and found their *reason to accuse Him* (see Luke 6:7). While they spewed and accused, Jesus *went off to the mountain to pray* (see Luke 6:12).

*But they themselves were filled with rage, and discussed together what they might do to Jesus (Luke 6:11).*

Praying throughout the night on the mountain was not a matter of escaping His enemies by taking a religious retreat. Jesus prayed all night to fight for His friends, without being distracted by His enemies.

All night on the mountain Jesus prayed and battled for the souls of twelve weak men. All would serve alongside of Him during His earthly ministry.

One would betray Him and another would deny Him. When He went to the Cross, all would desert Him but one. These Apostles would be privileged to follow Him on Earth and responsible to carry out His mission after He ascended into Heaven.

*And when day came, He called His disciples to Him and chose twelve of them, whom He also named as apostles (Luke 6:13).*

Jesus entered into prolonged and intense prayer before He selected "The Twelve." Praying through and after the selection of leaders within the Church would be a vast improvement over what most churches do to nominate and elect people to places of responsibility.

I was asked to complete an 18-part questionnaire sent by a Pastor Search Committee seeking a reference on behalf of a dear friend. Reading it was like waking up on the last day of school, and discovering a term paper I had forgotten to write. I am sure it was put together with all of the best intentions. But the flashing light on my dashboard was how little emphasis it placed on the prayer life of the next man who would lead this church. Only one of the 18 questions dealt with this vital area of leadership. Jesus placed a high priority on it. His Church should too!

A prayerful selection process must not be replaced by prayerless elections that are merely popularity contests. A prayerless process seldom discovers prayerful leaders, but it often empowers powerful politicians.

The mountain was a place of refuge, but it was not an escape hatch. Jesus went to the mountain to pray. He knew His enemies were active. Yet Jesus chose not to be defensive, but proactive. Turning His back on His enemies was not a way of running away from those who hated Him. Praying all night was His way of turning to His Father who loved Him.

The devil is an accuser. He throws the fiery darts of his accusations against the Father's children to see if they will stick. People who are constant critics and perpetual put-down artists do the devil's work. They may not be evil personified, but they are hand puppets of the evil one.

*At this time* (vs. 12) Jesus chose not to engage His enemies or escape them. He interceded for them. He never stopped. With His last breath on the Cross Jesus gasped out in prayer:

*"Father, forgive them; for they know not what they do"* (Luke 23:34 KJV).

Prolonged private prayer is the climate in which forgiveness towards your enemies is cultivated. Intercession for friends is rooted in the life of a prayer warrior. Jesus went to the mountain to pray, driven by the conspiracies of His enemies and His concern for the weaknesses of His friends.

Praying throughout the night Jesus turned His focus away from His enemies and towards the Father, while interceding on behalf of His friends. Prayer focuses on the Father's solution, not the enemy's pollution.

Jesus did not hide His head in the sand like the proverbial ostrich. He turned His eyes towards the Father in Heaven. Prolonged prayer enables you to focus on the Champion, in the middle of the battle, and not the enemy.

Praying throughout the day maintains your clear connection and consistent companionship with Jesus. Still, from the evidence of the Savior's life, there are times when prolonged periods of uninterrupted prayer are needed.

Breaking the power of the accuser is found by praying and entering into the presence of God.

Going to the mountain clears the air and your mind from the accusations and the conspiracies of the enemy. In the clamor and confusion created by the forces of evil, it is impossible for prayerless warriors to shout down the sound of the enemy camp.

Praying all night removed the voices of His accusers, and enabled Jesus to hear the voice of the Father. Praying will improve your hearing.

....................................

**NOTE TO SELF:** Whenever there is a crisis of leadership in the Church, in the city, or in the country, it is time to pray. Follow Jesus.

## TALK LESS! PRAY MORE!

# DISCERNMENT IS GOD'S CALL FOR INTERCESSION, NEVER TO FAULT FINDING.

OSWALD CHAMBERS

# 5

# THE 5,000

..................................

*Looking up toward heaven, He blessed the food,*
*and breaking the loaves He gave them to the disciples,*
*and the disciples gave them to the crowds* (Matthew 14:19).
(See also Mark 6:41, Luke 9:16, John 6:11.)

Giving thanks to God for the food provided by a young boy is the one common denominator in all four Gospel records of the miracle of *The Feeding of the Five Thousand.* Matthew, Mark, Luke, and John revealed that Jesus asked God's blessing on the food before distributing it to His disciples to pass on to the people.

John's account provides keen insight into the mind of Christ, and shows how His process always had a purpose. The Son pointed seekers to the Father as the source of their provision.

*A large crowd followed Him, because they saw the*
*signs which He was performing on those who were*
*sick . . . Therefore Jesus, lifting up His eyes and seeing*
*that a large crowd was coming to Him, said to Philip,*
*"Where are we to buy bread, so that these may eat?"*

*This He was saying to test him, for He Himself knew*
*what He was intending to do* (John 6:2, 5–6).

Jesus always does. Saying the blessing, giving thanks, or saying grace are all expressions of one of the earliest forms of prayer taught to a child. Children are not born with a streak of gratitude, but an attitude of entitlement. Wise parents teach their children to thank God for their food, but don't stop teaching their children how to pray, until their prayer life matures and develops into so much more. But I digress.

Three of the Gospel accounts record that Jesus looked toward Heaven before He prayed. The Bible does not mince words, nor does it waste words. Words mean things. Looking towards Heaven is not a throwaway line, but your lifeline to the source of answered prayer, the Father in Heaven.

When Jesus was asked by His disciples, *"Lord, teach us to pray,"* (see Luke 11:1) He began with the words, *"Our Father, who art in heaven"* (see Luke 11:2 KJV). Jesus turned to the Father in believing prayer whenever His life and ministry were on the line.

The Father's children follow His Son's lead into the arena of believing prayer, and look toward Heaven. If your life reveals no heart for prayer, you do not have the life of Jesus in your heart. Prayerless people full of themselves and not of the Spirit do not look toward Heaven, they wander into the tall grass searching for man-made answers to man-made problems. Prayerlessness never ends well.

*Most Christians pray sometimes, with some prayers*
*and some degree of perseverance, for some of God's*
*people. But to replace "some" with "all" in each*

29

*of these expressions would be to introduce us to a
new dimension of prayer.* —John R.W. Stott

*Praying at all times in the Spirit, with all
prayer and supplication. To that end keep alert
with all perseverance, making supplication
for all the saints* (Ephesians 6:18 ESV).

Jesus placed His disciples in an impossible situation, ON PURPOSE. This reveals the mind of Christ, the heart of God, and the purpose of prayer. Prayer is not about pleading with God to provide fair weather for the church picnic. Prayer is about turning the impossible into the HIMpossible.

*God's purpose for your life is to knock
you, out of you.* —Bill Stafford

Panic may not be the purest motive for believing prayer, but it is a great motivator for it. Coming to the end of your rope is not a call to make more rope. It is a call to pray. Jesus knew Philip was aware of prayer as a ritual and a sign of the righteous on feast days. He also knew Philip didn't believe prayer was the breath of life every day.

Jesus brought His disciples face-to-face with reality and pointed their eyes to the Father. The miracle of *The Feeding of the Five Thousand* was not the distribution of fish and bread, but the grace of God flowing into an impossible situation in the form of answered prayer.

I remember walking my 93-year-old father, Don Miller, back to his room at his retirement center when He softly spoke these words to me:

*Peace is the blessing of believing prayer.*

I can't put them into context, except to say, they were on his heart, and they came out of his mouth at a time I needed to hear them. Thank You Father for a praying dad.

When you are faced with an impossible crisis, a difficult choice, or an exasperating person, even believing prayer may begin in real panic, but it leads you to real peace. Peace does not come from the answer to a prayer, but from the blessing of the presence of the Father in the midst of the crisis, the choice, and the contrary. Where there is prayer, the Father is there.

Jesus faced the impossible by turning to the Father in prayer, and thanking Him for what He had already provided. A small boy's lunch was an unlikely source for a great miracle, but God sometimes delivers His greatest gifts in very small packages. A baby in a manger is the Father's signature statement on this truth.

Your attitude of gratitude releases the favor of the Father to step in and to do more than a prayerless person could ever imagine. Jesus prayed, the Father spread His favor, and the disciples fed the people. Believing prayer turns your panic into peace, and the impossible into the HIMpossible.

...............................

**NOTE TO SELF:** The sooner you get on board with what the Father has in mind for you, the sooner you will embrace prayer as part of His process for maturing you and not pampering you. Jesus knew exactly what He was doing when He asked one of His disciples to meet the needs of 5,000 people. Jesus knew the score, but He was looking for His disciples to get into the game. He still is. Are you ready?

# 6

# THE MOUNTAIN PART II

..............................

*And after He had sent the crowds away, He went up
on the mountain by Himself to pray; and when it was
evening, He was there alone* (Matthew 14:23).
(See also Mark 6:46, John 6:15.)

Lessons taught by Jesus in The School of Prayer are not so much studied in the classroom, as they are learned in the middle of a crisis. The School of Prayer is a war college where prayer warriors learn to lean on the Master by observing how He responded to the chaos and confusion around Him.

In August of 1973, I climbed Mt. Kilimanjaro in Tanzania, East Africa. The view of the world from the summit was spectacular, and the silence was eerily serene. All that could be heard was the crackling and falling of the ice on the glacier as the sun rose in the sky. Unknown to me was the impact climbing to 19,700 feet had on my body. When I returned to the lower elevations on the mountain, I no longer suffered with the same symptoms I had encountered on the previous three-day climb. My body had adapted to the discomfort by climbing higher, not by succumbing to it. Private prayer with the Father has the same kind of strengthening affect. It takes you above your comfort zone, and returns you to the war zone with strength you never knew you could have.

Your panic focuses on the disaster while prayer turns your eyes towards Jesus. The Master of all creation is also The Master of disaster, real or imagined.

Jesus extended an invitation to His disciples with a simple, yet profound statement, *"Follow Me"* (see Matthew 4:19). He offered His company to those seeking His Father's direction, protection, and correction. They were given an opportunity to leave what seemed hugely urgent to them, walk beside Him, and learn what was the most important lesson in life: *"Lord, teach us to pray"* (see Luke 11:1).

Take hold of what the Father has for you by letting go of what is already in your hands. Holding on to what looks like a security blanket can become a dangerous liability to your life of faith. Prayer releases false security and increases genuine faith.

In the middle of a successful ministry, Jesus withdrew from the clamor of the crowds, crying out to make Him King. He also left those closest to Him, to get alone with God. This record of the prayer life of Jesus indicates He sought the Father in the evening, as well as in the morning.

Jesus not only longed for intimate communication with His Father in the early morning hours, but during intense, all night sessions on the mountain. He was also drawn away from others and towards the Father to pray at the close of the day.

For those who put high priority on an early morning "quiet time," it is worth noting that Jesus was not only a morning person, but He was also an evening person. Apparently, there was not a time of the day that was more sacred to Him than the other, when it came to getting alone with the Father in prayer.

Corporate worship is highly valued in the contemporary church (as well it should be). From the earliest days of the Church, believers were warned about the dangers of turning their backs on assembling together to worship God. When sheep separate themselves from the flock, they become prey for predators of all kinds, inside and outside of the church.

Jesus placed a very high priority on getting away from the demands of the crowd, and praying with the Father, ALONE. He did not seek affirmation of His ministry from the crowd, but from the Father. He withdrew from those who wanted more from Him, and those who desired to be around Him.

Through private, personal prayer, He sought the company of the one who had called Him, not those who wanted to use or abuse Him.

Jesus refused to be tempted by the siren call of celebrity. He withdrew from the limelight of success, and stepped into the fading light of the day to get alone with the Father. You would be wise to follow His lead morning, noon, and night.

Preaching to the crowd, without hearing from God, may draw a crowd but fail to deliver God's message. Many start out as faithful messengers, but gradually stop speaking for God. While honing their communication skills, they start appeasing and appealing to the galleries. This never ends well.

Success and failure are team efforts, but too many preachers take them personally. The applause of celebrity stalkers, and the verbal abuse of critics can each drown out the voice of the Father. Anything that makes you place too high, or too low, a value on your ministry should be taken to the Father in prayer. This is best done as soon as the applause dies down, or your blood pressure goes up. You make the call.

Jesus let go of the crowds and left His disciples behind to get alone with the Father to pray. His purity was a reflection of His humility. Though He was God, the Son humbled Himself before the Father and yielded His will to pray and receive God's direction, protection, and correction.

> *Let this mind be in you, which was also in Christ Jesus: Who, being in the form of God, thought it not robbery to be equal with God: But made himself of no reputation, and took upon him the form of a servant, and was made in the likeness of men: And being found in fashion as a man, he humbled himself, and became obedient unto death, even the death of the cross. Wherefore God also hath highly exalted him, and given him a name which is above every name: That at the name of Jesus every knee should bow, of things in heaven, and things in earth, and things under the earth; And that every tongue should confess that Jesus Christ is Lord, to the glory of God the Father* (Philippians 2:5–11 KJV).

The prayerless do not have a heart for prayer because they have lost their minds. The sound of the applause of a great crowd or the abuse of a single critic can drown out the voice of the Spirit. Follow Jesus and get alone with the Father. Private personal prayer increases the sound of the still, small voice of His Spirit saying, "Can you hear Me now?"

..................................

**NOTE TO SELF:** You will either pray or you will be the prey. Private prayer is powerful because it separates you from the sound of the battle, and draws you nearer to the presence of the Champion. Prayer purifies your motives, and prepares you for more effective ministry. When the applause of the crowd becomes more important than the pause to pray, the time has come for your motives in ministry to be purified.

## TALK LESS! PRAY MORE!

GOD'S PURPOSE FOR YOUR LIFE
IS TO KNOCK YOU, OUT OF YOU.

BILL STAFFORD

# 7

# THE HAPPENING

..............................

*And it happened that while He was praying alone, the disciples were with Him, and He questioned them saying, "Who do the people say that I am?"* (Luke 9:18).

*And it happened* (vs. 18) seems like such an insignificant expression when it is separated from any close connection with the intense intercession Jesus carried out on behalf of His disciples. When Jesus prayed, it just so happened that power was released from Heaven.

As long as there is a math class, there will always be prayer in schools. My first experience with praying alone in a crowded room took place in my sixth grade math class at Mill Lane Junior High School in Farmingdale, New York. I had moved from Dallas, Texas to a city that was home to Republic Aviation. It built sophisticated fighter jets for the American military. The school system was highly influenced by the parents of my classmates who worked in the aerospace industry. I was in way over my head in my new math class, and I was calling out to God in silent prayer. The Supreme Court had recently determined prayer had no place in the classroom. I didn't care. It happened that I needed help. I prayed.

Jesus' intercession was the source of great insight and wisdom to His disciples. His early followers received far more favor from the Father than they ever knew. His grace did not come to them as a result of their eloquent prayers. It was granted to them due to the intimate and intense intercession of the Son. His grace always has, and always will be graded in answer to His prayers.

Since Jesus still intercedes for His followers, seated at the right hand of the Father, contemporary disciples continue to be the beneficiaries of the Son's intercession, and the Father's great favor. The Father's favor graced the early disciples and the Son's intercession remains the source of living hope and genuine faith in the lives of His contemporary followers. Thank You, Jesus, indeed.

When Jesus walked away from His temptation experience in the desert he had a clear insight into the purpose of Satan. The evil one wished Him no good will. What the enemy did to the Son, he would do to His friends.

The three temptations from Satan convinced Jesus to prepare His disciples for what they would face. The simple truth is everything in life is a faith test.

***While He was praying alone, the disciples were with Him.*** At first glance, this passage of Scripture appears to be a contradiction of terms and a physical impossibility. It is neither.

After the miracle of *The Feeding of the Five Thousand*, Jesus prayed alone for His disciples. Carrying the twelve baskets of leftovers must have been a powerful reminder to the disciples of what they had just witnessed. As they walked and talked about what they had seen God do in the past, they were in danger of missing out on intimacy with the Son in the present tense.

*You can't live on yesterday's manna.* —Unknown Author

One of the greatest mistakes you can make is dropping your guard after a great spiritual victory. The counter attack of the enemy is often swift and devastating if you are unprepared. Jesus prayed because He knew the enemy always preyed on the unsuspecting.

The intercession of Jesus took place as He journeyed down the road with His disciples. His body was near them, but His heart was drawn towards Heaven. Prayer was the Son's homing beacon, or His spiritual GPS. Prayer connected Him to the Father. Jesus was alone with the Father, and at the same time, was able to pray on a dusty road surrounded by His unguarded disciples.

Jesus prayed privately and publicly. General crowd noise is generally an annoyance, and it often distracts your wandering mind from a private conversation with the Father. Rather than allowing it to impede His intercession, Jesus used it as a catalytic converter for prayer. Prepare to do it, too.

Praying alone, the disciples were with Him. Overhearing His disciples did not prove to be a distraction to Jesus. Their conversation fueled His attraction to the Father.

*Discernment is God's call for intercession, never to fault finding.* —Oswald Chambers

Jesus prayed and expected results. Praying was not a devotional exercise that provided Him some information about the Father. Intercession was personal and private conversation with the Father. When Jesus prayed, He expected to be heard.

He expected the Father to respond and His disciples to receive answers to His prayers on their behalf. Jesus knew exactly who He was. When He questioned His disciples, He was not looking for information from them. He was expecting the results of His intercession for them.

Intercession is not about changing the will of the Father. It is more about preparing your ears to hear and softening your heart to receive the will of the Father.

*He questioned them saying, "Who do the people say that I am?"* Peter answered, *"The Christ of God"* (vs. 20). Jesus followed this response with a warning, *"not to tell this to anyone"* (vs. 21).

One right answer does not guarantee a believer will be right about everything. Jesus prayed, and Peter heard from God once. Peter received Who Jesus was, but he would have a harder time grasping where Jesus went (the Cross). Still, Jesus prayed for Peter until his mind was clear and his faith restored.

Jesus is still praying for you to hear from the Father, yield to His will, and receive His direction, protection, and correction. Jesus is never more WITH His disciples than when He is ALONE with the Father. Your believing prayer involves listening to and obeying the Father, not listing requests and instructing the Father.

..............................

**NOTE TO SELF:** The next time you hear more crowd noise than the still, small voice of the Spirit, start praying for those around you to hear from the Father. What you hear others say will either become a distraction or a source of discernment. If it is the latter, then it is a call to pray for people, not criticize them.

## TALK LESS! PRAY MORE!

# 8

# THE TRANSFIGURATION

...............................

*Some eight days after these sayings, He took along Peter and John and James, and went up to the mountain to pray. And while He was praying, the appearance of His face became different, and His clothing became white and gleaming* (Luke 9:28–29).

After the miracle of *The Feeding of the Five Thousand*, Jesus challenged all of His disciples with the very essence of a walk with God. He invited them to follow Him up to the mountain to pray.

A personal walk with God begins with immediate and personal obedience to the words of Jesus, *"Follow Me"* (see Matthew 4:19). This new Christian walk continues by also applying the testimony of the Apostle Paul, *I die daily* (see 1 Corinthians 15:31). A balanced walk takes both.

> *"If anyone wishes to come after Me, he must deny himself, and take up his cross and follow Me."* —Jesus (Matthew 16:24)

Eight days after making this statement, once again, Jesus went up to the mountain to pray. Some people climb higher to get a better view of creation available to them by a change in elevation. Jesus was drawn to greater heights to get a better view of the Creator. A closer view of God requires more than a change in elevation, it requires a focus on intimate communication with the Father and intense intercession on behalf of others.

Luke records that this time Jesus did not go alone to pray, but took three of His closest friends with Him. Receiving the message does not require repeating the miracle on *The Mount of Transfiguration*. To learn the lessons of the experience, they must first be remembered and then received.

A miracle is a sign of more to come, not a point of the final arrival at the destination. In Luke 9:18, after Jesus fed the 5,000, He gave His twelve disciples a one question pop quiz: *"Who do the people say that I am?"* Peter's correct response was, *"The Christ of God"* (vs. 20). Jesus then challenged each of His disciples wishing to follow Him, to *"deny himself, and take up his cross daily"* (vs. 23).

Dying daily requires a living faith that is sustained by believing prayer. Your death is exhibited by praying with the last breath in your lungs and by climbing higher with your next step of faith.

Climbing higher requires leaving other people behind and former pastimes below. Peter, John, and James left the other disciples behind and followed Jesus to new heights. What they were privileged to see on the mountain was not a result of their experience or their eloquence. It was a by-product of their obedience.

*It is not well for a man to pray cream and*
*live skim milk.* —Henry Ward Beecher

*And while He was praying* (vs. 29) indicates that Jesus didn't just climb the mountain to get a better view—He climbed higher to get in touch with God. Make an effort to go to church, attend a conference, a camp, and even a prayer meeting, but don't fail to get in touch with God. Don't skim the surface of God's Word and fail to taste the cream of His presence. Jesus had a taste for what mattered most in His life, and through prayer, He dove into the deeper and sweeter presence of the Father.

Prayer made a visible difference in Jesus because the Father reached down and touched Him. When Jesus knelt down and called out to the Father, He responded with His presence. Prayerless people exhibit a form of insanity by continuing to expect a different result by repeating the same mistake.

Prayerful people experience the difference only God can make.

*The appearance of His face became different* (vs. 29).

During the past 45 years of ministry, I have presided over the deathwatches and funerals of hundreds of people. Those who are in the final hours of their lives on Earth take on a different look, as they gain a clearer perspective on Heaven. It has not been unusual for people to call out by name to people they recognize, but who remain unseen by others in the room.

Believing prayer has a similar effect. It puts you above the sound of the battle, and in touch with the Champion who has already won the victory. The faces of those who pray are not marked with worry lines, but their faces reflect the peace which passes all understanding (see Philippians 4:7).

*His clothing became white and gleaming* (vs. 29).

One of the earliest Madison Avenue platitudes I can recall is, "Clothes make the man." It isn't true. Actually, clothes only announce the man. What the man does while wearing the clothes makes or breaks him. Better clothes won't make a better man. The prayerless man is merely the "poster boy" of an empty suit. Cheap grace always produces cheap suits.

The appearance of Jesus, both His face and His clothes, changed while He was praying. This was a reflection of the Father's pleasure on His Son. The followers of Jesus are never more pleasing to the Father than when they follow His Son into the arena of prayer. Self-made men are prayerless men who make a name for themselves but never discover the difference God can make in them and through them.

*And while He was praying . . . two men were talking with Him; and they were Moses and Elijah, who, appearing in glory, were speaking of His departure which He was about to accomplish at Jerusalem (vs. 29–31).*

Waking from prayerless sleep and seeing Moses and Elijah, Peter (never one to fail to speak His mind), called on Jesus to mark this special occasion with three equal tabernacles. He equated these two men talking with Jesus as a sign of their equality with Him. *Not realizing what he was saying* (vs. 33), Peter was silenced by the voice of God: *"This is My Son, My Chosen One; listen to Him"* (vs. 35).

Dying daily involves following Jesus into the arena of prayer and staying there long enough until your concern for change in your circumstances pales in significance to your desire for the change only the presence of God can make in your countenance. The Father knows by the look on your face when you have been worrying more and praying less. Other people can tell the difference, too. Die daily. Worry less.

..................................

**NOTE TO SELF:** When God allows you to be a part of something only He can do, it is not an excuse for you to sit down and take a break, or to write your memoirs. It is an invitation to die daily and to climb higher in your walk with Jesus. Get over yourself and get with the Father, in the Spirit, by praying in the name of the Son, Jesus Christ.

## TALK LESS! PRAY MORE!

PRAYER IS NOT A MATTER OF
CHANGING THINGS EXTERNALLY,
BUT ONE OF WORKING MIRACLES
IN A PERSON'S INNER NATURE.

OSWALD CHAMBERS

# 9

# THE REVEALED

..................................

*At that time Jesus said, "I praise You, Father, Lord of heaven and earth, that You have hidden these things from the wise and intelligent and have revealed them to infants. Yes, Father, for this way was well-pleasing in Your sight (Matthew 11:25–26). (See also Luke 10:21.)*

Jesus denounced the cities that had seen most of His miracles, but had failed to repent. The Son pronounced judgment on *"the wise and intelligent,"* (vs. 25) because they failed to yield to the Father and allow the Spirit to turn their lives around.

*You need to get the best education you can, and get over it as soon as possible.* —Dr. Chuck Swindoll

This may be my favorite quote of this great Bible teacher. His words are so spot on when it comes to the proper perspective I need to maintain regarding any insight I may have gained through my own personal study. The Father has the capacity to reveal what I claim to know to infants. A keen mind, honed by a good education, should never lead to a big head.

The words of Jesus remind me that a humble and childlike heart leads to a teachable spirit.

Your unbroken, childish pride is neither softened nor satisfied by a great work of God. It only responds to the Father with a spirit of entitlement demanding, "What else ya' got?"

Scripture reveals time and again, a timeless truth that *Jesus Loves the Little Children*. The early childhood song by C. Herbert Woolston, taught in Sunday School, was theologically sound:

> *Jesus loves the little children,*
> *All the children of the world.*
> *Red and yellow, black and white,*
> *They are precious in His sight.*
> *Jesus loves the little children of the world.*

They are precious in His sight, indeed (see Matthew 19:14). Stay with me on this. The slight sprinkling of a faithless child has about as much power to convert or turn a life around as the full immersion of a prideful adult. The power to save is released when genuine humility is expressed. Jesus set this standard for citizenship in His preamble to the constitution of Kingdom in Matthew 5:

> *"Blessed are the poor in spirit, for theirs*
> *is the kingdom of heaven"* (vs. 3).

The blessing was not pronounced on poor people, but humble people. Prideful people simply don't want to have their lives turned around. Instead of allowing the Spirit of God to convert them into genuine believers, they create excuses for their incorrigible behavior. In the words of Dr. Phil, "How's that workin' for ya?"

My personal belief in Scripture leads me to embrace the symbol of immersion as the clearest expression of a turnaround in a believer's life. I have always pronounced over the baptismal candidate, "I baptize you in the name of the Father, the Son, and the Holy Spirit."

The help to turn your life around does not come from a healthy helping of water, but from the Helper. The Holy Spirit only enters into *"the poor in spirit."* Yielding to the symbol of baptism without obeying the leading of the Spirit robs the symbol of its true meaning, and doesn't give any evidence of a turnaround in your life.

Being buried beneath the water should lead you to listen and walk in the Spirit. Words mean things, and when you are raised up out of the water, the first words you hear are: "Buried with Christ in baptism. Raised to walk in newness of life."

Immersion symbolizes salvation as a turnaround of the living dead into living converts. A humbled, changed life is what salvation is really all about. Anything less than a turnaround conversion is only a slow dance of personal rebellion.

> *"Truly I say to you, unless you are converted and become like children, you will not enter the kingdom of heaven. Whoever then humbles himself as this child, he is the greatest in the kingdom of heaven"* (Matthew 18:2–4).

Genuine humility is not a matter of thinking less of oneself, but of thinking of oneself less. Prayerless people are so prideful they cannot bring themselves to yield to the Father's direction, protection, or correction. Jesus offers His yoke, the Spirit provides the fruit of Christ's character, but still, the prideful chafe under the yoke and offer imitation fruit. Never be too proud to pray.

Jesus praised His Father for hiding His presence and the power to repent from the prideful. The Father only reveals Himself to His humble children of faith and He offers the name of His Son as the key to His presence. Pray and never hesitate to obey. This is what it's all about.

Prayerful, humble repentance is the sign and substance of a changed life. Baptism is only the symbol of it. Being sprinkled, immersed, or dry-cleaned won't turn a rebellious life around. Prayer takes the stiffness out of your neck and your tendency to chafe under the yoke of Jesus. Prayer will soften your hard heart to receive the fruit and bear the character of Christ that only the Spirit can produce.

Approach the Father as a little child dependent upon Him for life and love. Spoiled brats demand what they want. Humble children receive what He gives. When you let go of what you want, the Father reveals what you need the most, a personal turnaround. Never substitute total immersion for complete conversion or settle for anything less.

...............................

**NOTE TO SELF:** Don't be fooled by the song, the *Hokey Pokey*. Doing what you want is not "what it's all about."

## TALK LESS! PRAY MORE!

# 10

# THE PLACE

..............................

*It happened that while Jesus was praying in a certain place, after He had finished, one of His disciples said to Him, "Lord, teach us to pray just as John also taught his disciples" (Luke 11:1).*

One of the most underrated statements in Scripture may very well be, *It happened.* Authors of fantasy literature are known to introduce their story lines with, "Once upon a time." Luke begins his record of this vital turning point in history, not with a flight of fancy, but with a statement of fact: *It happened.*

The prayer life of the followers of Jesus is based upon this one solid truth: Long before prayer warriors ever start praying to Him, Jesus has been praying for them. When Jesus prays, things happen that turn the impossible into the HIMpossible. He only needs one person of faith to begin the Spiritual transformation in the heart of an individual, or the soul of a nation. Be the one.

The Son's intense intimacy with the Father and His intercession for His followers have never been a devotional detour from the cares of the world or the current crisis of the hour.

Intercession has always been an expression of His clear perspective on what is required to make a difference in the world and to meet the need of the hour: PRAYER to the Father.

Wherever and whenever the Spirit ignites the fire of prayer in the hearts of believers, it is a result of the Son's intimacy with the Father, and His intercession for His Church. Those who have a passion for prayer need not take pride in it. They should be humbled by the very idea that they have been entrusted with the stewardship of this powerful weapon. No man or woman came up with the idea of praying. Prayer is not a good idea—it's God's idea. And if people are doing it, the idea came to them, while Jesus was praying.

Jesus set a priority, made a pattern, and chose a place for prayer. He wore out a path for intimacy with the Father and intercession for His Church. His disciples knew He could be found praying, in a certain place.

Prayer warriors who intend to take a stand against the enemy need a place to kneel. Homes and churches are filled with chairs, rooms, or special places that meet specific needs. Without a kitchen there wouldn't be much effective cooking done in a home. Just as without carving out a place and a time to pray, there will be little praying. People seek out places to improve their physical health, but often fail to care for their spiritual health. Do both.

Anyone seeking a crowd to join them in prayer will either be too intimidated by the prospect of an empty room that they will cancel the prayer meeting, or they will be very disappointed by the turnout of those who showed up to pray. Luke 11:1 indicates, one solitary person can make a huge difference:

*One of His disciples said to Him, "Lord, teach us to pray."*

51

It is interesting to note that Jesus was not met by a delegation of disciples—only one came to Him and said, *"Lord, teach us to pray."* It only takes one praying person to begin the next Great Awakening.

Be the one! Stop looking for a crowd . . . start praying. No one can follow you until they see the pattern in your own life, your home, your church, your community, and your country. Get over yourself. It only takes one prune to start a movement. Be the one!

> *The effective, fervent prayer of a righteous*
> *man avails much* (James 5:16 NKJV).

At a recent retirement party, my father was asked to share his favorite verse of Scripture. Without hesitation, he responded, "Lord, teach us to pray."

After three decades of traveling to six continents and to over 1,000 churches in the United States teaching people to pray, this is the one verse the Spirit of God continues to illuminate in my dad's heart. Even through the fog of a fading memory, it still rises like the dawn and comes to his mind, bringing clarity of thought and a purpose for life. I'm grateful to my dad for being the one who has always led the way to prayer in my life and in the lives of thousands of other people whose names are known only to the Father.

In 1873, in Dublin, Ireland, American preacher Dwight L. Moody heard these words spoken to him by a dear friend, Henry Varley, a British revivalist:

> *The world has yet to see what God will do*
> *with a man fully consecrated to him.*

Moody spent the rest of his life focused on yielding his own heart to God and leaving the results up to Him. To this day, he is still remembered for huge crowds hungering for his great-hearted preaching.

If the next Great Awakening hinges on one person's heart being placed in the hands of the Father, will you be the one? One praying person is worth more to the Father than the world could ever produce. Be the one who finds the time and the place to come to the Son, and say with all your heart, "Lord, teach us to pray."

................................

**NOTE TO SELF:** Can the people closest to you find the time when, and the place where, you pray? Let those closest to you know you have a prayer closet, and that you use it on their behalf.

## TALK LESS! PRAY MORE!

# 11

# THE TEACHER

...............................

*"Lord, teach us to pray"* (Luke 11:1).

If the one disciple who made this request of Jesus had known the consequences of what he was asking, the request may have never been made. There is a big difference between learning "to pray" and knowing "how to pray."

One of the more surreal experiences I have ever had in 45 years of ministry is the invitation I received to lead a marriage enrichment retreat while I was still a single adult. I don't know who took the greater leap of faith. It may have been me by accepting the invitation. It was probably those couples who came to the retreat in search of help. I prepared diligently, I read every book I could find on marriage, and came equipped with every communication technique recommended. I knew a lot about the concept of marriage, but I had never been married. Big difference.

Thankfully, I survived. Most of their marriages did too. I still can't believe I did it. But I digress.

An educated nutritionist is not always the healthiest person in the room. Knowing the right things to eat but eating the wrong things, is counterproductive to real nutrition, yet many experts still do it. Some politicians say, "Knowledge is power." Where prayer is concerned, knowledge is not enough. When you know the power of prayer, you have not just learned about it, theologically, you have experienced it, personally.

Studying, preaching, talking, singing, and writing about prayer are not the same things as engaging in prayer. Experience is one of the great teachers of prayer. You do not know the power of prayer until you have learned "to pray." Prayer warriors know "how to pray" and "when to pray." Do both.

*Experience: that most brutal of teachers.*
*But you learn, my God do you learn.* —C. S. Lewis

Using every current crisis as the catalytic converter for more intensive prayer lowers it to the level of crisis management. This habit robs a prayer warrior of the joy of prayer as intimate communication between the Heavenly Father and His child. There may be intense prayer generated during a crisis, but it never rises to the level of intimacy Jesus found when praying to the Father.

When the disciples heard Jesus pray, at least one of them must have sensed a distinct difference. Jesus did not run to His Father out of a sense of sheer panic or a sense of spiritual obligation. He prayed in order to maintain intimate communication with the Father.

Through prayer, Jesus found the power to yield His will to the Father's. He prayed long enough until He could say with His words and express with His life: *"Not My will, but Yours be done"* (see Luke 22:42).

Jesus is still the great Teacher of prayer, and in The School of

Prayer, there is one great lesson of prayer you must master. In one word, the lesson is: YIELD.

> *To say that "prayer changes things" is not as close to the truth as saying, "Prayer changes me and then I change things." God has established things so that prayer, on the basis of redemption, changes the way a person looks at things. Prayer is not a matter of changing things externally, but one of working miracles in a person's inner nature.* —Oswald Chambers

To soar to new heights in prayer, stop praying parakeet like prayers, perpetually peeping, Me! Me! Me! Life-changing prayer transforms ME into THEE. The prayer life of Jesus teaches this great lesson—He focused on the Father and sought His direction, protection, and correction for God's purpose in His life. Before Jesus won His victory at the Cross, He surrendered to the Father in "The Battle of the Will."

The Teacher still leads you to pray, "Thy will be done." Learn the lesson and discover the joy.

..............................

**NOTE TO SELF:** One question clarifies who the teacher of prayer really is in your life. The question: When do you pray the most? The answer: When things are going wrong, not so much when things are going right. Right answer. Wrong decision. Change.

## TALK LESS! PRAY MORE!

# 12

# THE REQUEST

..............................

*"Lord, teach us to pray"* (Luke 11:1).

This simple statement in Luke 11:1, brought to Jesus by one soul-starved disciple, unleashed the greatest weapon in the battle against evil that you will ever have available to you this side of Heaven. Your request will never be ignored by the Lord Jesus Christ. Whatever you bring to Him, it is always answered.

Shortly after I enrolled in first grade, at O.M. Roberts Elementary School, I was taught to print my name in block letters on a Big Chief tablet with a huge blue pencil. The drill called for each of us to scrawl our name over and over again until it became legible enough for our teacher, Miss Hamm, to recognize. She walked around the room looking over our shoulders, giving us encouragement, and checking our progress. Sammie, my classmate to my left, was cheating off of my paper. When Miss Hamm yanked him up from his desk by the suspenders of his overalls, he gave me a threatening look. He was convinced I had ratted him out. Poor Sammie, he wasn't the sharpest knife in the drawer.

In The School of Prayer it is not permitted to cheat off of someone else's paper. The Teacher always knows who has been doing it. Don't stay after school. Learn to pray.

When you are humble enough to admit you do not know it all you will be enrolled in The School of Prayer and taught, to pray. When you confess you are in need, you will not only receive instruction about prayer—you will be inspired to pray. There is no graduation day on Earth from The School of Prayer. The lessons of intercession are learned on Earth until the student graduates to Heaven. The only degree offered or awarded is a Ph.D. (Pray Hard Daily).

The power of prayer is found in the presence of the Lord. Jesus makes Himself available to you when you honor His Lordship and desire His companionship. Those who are proud of their education and eloquence may talk about Him—yet fail to talk to Him.

Talking about marriage and being married are not the same thing. In a similar way, talking about Jesus, without talking to Him falls short of intimacy with the Lord.

When David walked through the valley of the shadow of death, he discovered a life-changing truth: *You are with me* (Psalm 23:4). Until that moment in time, David's 23rd Psalm had been filled with solid references about the Lord. When fear overwhelmed him and danger surrounded him, David's communication was transformed from a third person view of God to a face-to-face conversation with Him. Believing prayer does that . . . EVERY TIME. There is always a great danger in being trapped in the *valley of the shadow of death* (see Psalm 23:4). The enemy sets an ambush for those who become too busy doing the work of the Lord, that they fail to spend time with the Lord of the work.

> *Beware of any work for God that causes or allows*
> *you to avoid concentrating on Him. A great num-*
> *ber of Christian workers worship their work. The*
> *only concern of Christian workers should be their*
> *concentration on God.* —Oswald Chambers

The enemy always knows the difference long before the weary worker is aware of the loss of power. The enemy fears the presence of the Champion, not the frantic efforts of the foot soldier.

One disciple heard something in the prayer life of the Lord that was missing in his own life and those around him. Recognizing one's need always launches the request and unleashes the weapon of prayer. Praying by blowing the whistle on others may appear gratifying, but it always invites the Lord's correction of the whistle-blower.

> *Until the church owns prayer as a world-class weapon in*
> *the battle against evil and cherishes prayer as a means*
> *of intimate and constant communication with God, the*
> *turnaround efforts of a body are severely limited, if not*
> *altogether doomed, to failure.* —George Barna

**"LORD"** expresses a heart of humility and a spirit of total surrender to the way and the will of Jesus. Prayerless people are prideful people. Only the humble of heart will truly know His presence and His power. Heaven on Earth and in each heart always begins with, *"Blessed are the poor in spirit"* (Matthew 5:3).

**"TEACH"** reveals the process of prayer. The School of Prayer only enrolls those who admit they don't know it all. English theologian and commentator, Dr. William Barclay, was once asked if a certain young man was one of his students. He replied, "No. He only attends my classes." His point was clear. Sitting in class with a stiff-necked rebellion to what is being taught only postpones graduation. Rebellious behavior always results in having to stay after school, or repeating the course.

**"US"** unveils the essence of believing prayer, intercession. The request was made by a single person on behalf of a corporate body. Intercessory prayer is the very heartbeat of the Lord. He sits at the right hand of the Father and intercedes for His followers at this very moment. Those who follow Him not only have Jesus in their hearts, but they share His heartbeat and compassion for others. Selfish, self-centered prayers may very well be answered, but they always fall short of the kind of intimacy and intercession that marks the prayer life of Jesus.

**"TO PRAY"** completes the point of the statement. Prayer doesn't take place by listing requests and sharing needs. Anyone who has ever led a Wednesday night prayer meeting or an opening assembly in a Senior Adult Sunday School Department is very familiar with "the gasp" that escapes the mouths of those who have heard the latest ghastly hospital report on those who are missing from the gathering. The point of the meeting seems to be telling the goriest story, not interceding for their relief. In the words of a Texas rancher who knew how to tell a tall tale: "The first liar never has a chance." Stop it! Start praying!

...................................

**NOTE TO SELF:** Pray it, don't say it. Saying it over and over again, and putting it before people, without laying it before Jesus, is not praying. Taking it to Jesus and putting it before the people is not always the same thing. Whatever you share, make sure it begins and ends in prayer. Anything less is not intercession. Sharing without praying only postpones the solution. Warning: You must be prepared to be changed before you see a change in others.

## TALK LESS! PRAY MORE!

# 13

# THE 4,000

..............................

*And He took the seven loaves and the fish; and giving thanks, He broke them and started giving them to the disciples, and the disciples gave them to the people* (Matthew 15:36). (See also Mark 8:6–7.)

Manley Beasley was a great man of faith. He walked among Southern Baptists giving them more insight into God's faith-building process than most people ever wanted to know. He would often pose one of his favorite questions to preachers and anyone else seeking a deeper life with Christ: "What are you trusting God for today?"

I remember vividly the first time, Bro. Manley asked me that question. I had invited him to preach to my people, and I expected him to have a word for them, not for me. It was always a surprise whenever my hired gun turned and put his sights on me. I never saw it coming.

Bro. Manley's question was meant to take a person to a whole new level of trust in God. His point was to press believers to understand the full measure of faith and their lack of confidence in it. This kind of faith is not a doctrinal position, but a dynamic passion. He wanted to know if people were trusting God for something so impossible and improbable, that if God didn't come through, they were toast.

Jesus did not protect His disciples from the impossible or the improbable. He confronted them with their lack of faith over and over again. His questions were designed to bring them to the end of their own resources and to learn to rely on Him as the source.

Faith is not figuring out what man can do and financing it as cheap as possible. Faith is facing an impossible crisis and probable failure with a calm and confidence in God to perform the improbable, and to provide the HIMpossible. Big difference!

Fear posing as faith causes you to protect your reputation by not expecting too much out of God in public. When you dilute faith to a form of piety, it only allows enough elbowroom for you to do what you are able to do in your own strength, with your own resources.

At the completion of a task, the protected and the pious engage in an awkward, disingenuous balancing act of giving God the glory, while taking credit for the accomplishment. The contemporary church is often marked, by underwhelming results being claimed by people with overwhelming egos. It is not a pretty picture, and the world is not impressed by the show. Stop it!

Jesus questioned the disciples' faith regularly to test if they were improving in their dependence on Him, or leaning on their own wisdom and creativity. Prior to *The Feeding of the Four Thousand*, Jesus stated in Matthew 15:

> *"I feel compassion for the people . . . and I do not want to send them away hungry . . ."* The disciples said to Him, *"Where would we get so many loaves in this desolate place to satisfy such a large crowd?"* And Jesus said to them, *"How many loaves do you have?"* (vs. 32–34).

The disciples were frustrated by the compassion of Jesus, not a hungry crowd of people. Up until the time Jesus spoke about His passion to meet the need of 4,000 people, the disciples had their bases covered. They had seven loaves and some fish, and were more than willing to share it among themselves. They were focused on survival. But Jesus was interested in revival. He still is.

Revival takes place when your fear of failure dies and your life-giving faith is resurrected. Jesus intended to bring His disciples to the end of their resources by having them come face-to-face with the impossibility of meeting the need. Jesus didn't intend to lower His expectations for His disciples. He focused on raising their level of trust in Him. He still does.

Jesus felt compassion for the people. Feeding them was a natural by-product of His concern for them. The disciples were proud of their association with Jesus, but when asked to share His compassion, they were intimidated. They counted what they had in their hands and trusted in their own resources to meet the need, not Jesus.

*The Feeding of the Four Thousand* might be more accurately described as "The Faith-building of the Twelve." Faced with the impossible, the disciples eventually placed what they had in the hands of Jesus, and Jesus performed the improbable and provided the HIMpossible.

..................................

**NOTE TO SELF:** Believing prayer faces your fear of failure, by placing any minor inconvenience and every impossible crisis in the hands of Jesus. Believing prayer leans on Jesus to handle it with care. When faced with the fear of failure and in need of resurrected faith, HANDLE WITH PRAYER. Don't settle for survival. Expect revival. Questioning your faith is not always a sign of disbelief in God. It is often an expression of distrust in yourself, or the fear of failure.

## TALK LESS! PRAY MORE!

UNTIL THE CHURCH OWNS PRAYER AS A WORLD-CLASS WEAPON IN THE BATTLE AGAINST EVIL AND CHERISHES PRAYER AS A MEANS OF INTIMATE AND CONSTANT COMMUNICATION WITH GOD, THE TURNAROUND EFFORTS OF A BODY ARE SEVERELY LIMITED, IF NOT ALTOGETHER DOOMED, TO FAILURE.

GEORGE BARNA

# 14

# THE CHILDREN

..............................

*Then some children were brought to Him so that He might lay His hands on them and pray; and the disciples rebuked them. But Jesus said, "Let the children alone, and do not hinder them from coming to Me; for the kingdom of heaven belongs to such as these." After laying His hands on them, He departed from there* (Matthew 19:13–15). (See also Mark 10:15–16 and Luke 18:15.)

Two common denominators in each of these passages is the disciples' open rebuke of the children and the Master's personal touch on them. The rebuke of the children revealed the content of the hearts of the disciples. The rebuke of the disciples revealed the character of Jesus. Follow Him!

One of my favorite days as a pastor was the opportunity to conduct Parent/Baby Dedication Sundays. These occasions were always filled with the excitement of a tightrope walker working without a net. You never knew what was going to happen, and the children rarely followed the script. Still, these days were always filled with prayer and promise, and I could sense the pleasure of the Son as we welcomed little ones into the world.

The disciples appointed themselves as gatekeepers to the Kingdom. Rather than positioning themselves as welcome mats to the Master, they were elbowing each other (and little ones) for a seat on the front row of the class. Jesus took them to school and put them back in their place, in the back of the class.

*"Do not hinder them from coming to Me"* (Matthew 19:14).

One of the first songs I learned in Sunday School was *Jesus Loves the Little Children*. It clearly reveals the heart of Jesus and the worldwide embrace of His global compassion. As the contemporary church gathers for worship, it is crucial to pray for God's protection of His little ones. Christian children around the world are being beheaded, buried alive, kidnapped, and sold into slavery by Islamic extremists.

*Jesus loves the little children, all the children of the world.*
*Red and yellow, black and white, they are precious in*
*His sight. Jesus loves the little children of the world.*

The disciples fell into the trap of people who exert themselves to do more for Jesus, but end up expressing less of Him. The disciples may have had good intentions, but they missed God's best. Jesus set the record straight and revealed the love of the Father for the children.

The prayer life of Jesus reveals He prayed to the Father until His heart was filled with the Father's will and way to carry out ministry. The disciples were proud of their position on Team Jesus. In their own eyes, they had been promoted as men in authority—they were so close, yet so far away.

Prayer warriors are not marked by a passion for being in authority, but they exhibit a persistent humility to be under authority. This is where the power of prayer is found by the humble—and when it is released through them, it mystifies the proud.

Prideful people hold onto a position of authority only to find out they have no power. Prayerful people yield to the Father's authority and discover the Spirit's life-changing, life-giving power, in the name of the Son.

Prayer softens the heart of the humble to embrace those whom the Father loves. Prayerlessness hardens a heart until there is very little flow of the Father's love to those who need it the most. The Spirit's mark on the heart of a disciple of Jesus is the love of the Father (see Galatians 5:22–23).

Prayerless people may hold themselves in high regard, and even hold what appears to be an exalted position in the Kingdom. Yet their private prayerlessness only invites the public rebuke of the Father. Jesus rebuked the disciples for grasping for a position close to Him without taking hold of the hands of little children and bringing them to Him.

"Setting the woods on fire" in ministry sometimes brings the heat, but sheds very little light. One thing is certain—prayerless people are blinded by the smoke of man-made ministry, and breathe in their own toxic ether until they can't see *"the least of these"* (Matthew 25:45) or say an encouraging word to anyone.

There is no record of the words Jesus prayed over the children, only the repeated images of His tenderness toward them. My personal favorite is:

*And He took them in His arms and began blessing them, laying His hands on them* (Mark 10:16).

There is something about this gentle picture that warms my heart and tenderizes it to the point of surrendering my will to the Father's will. It encourages me to put on my ministry eyes and become more aware of opportunities to minister, pray for, and bless those who have no power to advance my own personal agenda or return the favor to me.

I find myself called to pray for parents who have such a powerful responsibility to bring their children to Jesus. The little children, recorded in these Scripture passages who received a touch and a blessing from Jesus, were brought to Him by parents and guardians who wished the best for their little ones during the worst of times. Wise parents still do. Pray for them, and encourage them.

...............................

**NOTE TO SELF:** Your ministry-hardened heart is a poor substitute for the compassion of Jesus. Sometimes the bright stage lights of an active, public ministry have a way of evaporating from your heart the one thing that is most important in ministry, the heart of the Father. Prayer protects your heart from being consumed by ministry and fills you with the Father's love for people. Do it!

## TALK LESS! PRAY MORE!

# 15

# THE FAITHFUL

..............................

*But I have prayed for you, that your faith may not fail; and you, when once you have turned again, strengthen your brothers"* (Luke 22:32).

Self-appointed leaders and Spirit-anointed leaders have one thing in common: Each can be tempted to become full of S.E.L.F. (Selfish Egos Living Freely).

One of the more intriguing passages of Scripture is found in the statement made to Simon Peter prior to Jesus informing His leading disciple of His personal intercession for him. Jesus said, *"Simon, Simon, behold, Satan has demanded permission to sift you like wheat"* (Luke 22:31).

In understanding the intent of the content of Scripture, context is everything. Jesus had just overheard *a dispute among them as to which of them was regarded to be the greatest* (Luke 22:24).

Apparently Peter's over-active ego was not the only one running amuck among the twelve disciples. Any claim Peter had on being the greatest among the disciples was disputed and debated—Jesus stepped in to clear the air:

*"But the one who is the greatest among you must become like the youngest, and the leader like the servant. For who is greater, the one who reclines at the table or the one who serves? Is it not the one who reclines at the table? But I am among you as the one who serves"* (Luke 22:26–27).

The price of leadership and the cost of discipleship are equally expensive. They each require death to self. When Jesus heard His disciples discussing how valuable they were to the Kingdom, Jesus specifically reminded Peter of the price on his head and the target on his back.

One of the greatest tributes made to a faithful man, Sir Robert Shirley, is found, appropriately enough, carved in stone over the entrance to a small chapel he built on his estate in England in 1653. He did so during a time when it was not politically correct to identify himself with the Church of England. His refusal to support the regime in power led to his imprisonment and the loss of his life. The price he paid was not forgotten. The inscription over the chapel entrance pays tribute to his faithfulness in part with these words: "Sir Robert Shirley . . . whose singular praise it is to have done the best things in ye worst of times."

In the book of Job, all hell was unleashed on the hero of the story, right after God had bragged about him. Satan challenged the value of Job's virtue and the purity of his motives. Spoiler Alert: God allowed the evil one to put both to the test. Even with a happy ending, it was not a pretty picture. It rarely is. Jesus warned His disciples about laying claim to the role of a leader based upon the world's value system. In His Kingdom, the servant is held in the highest esteem: *"The greatest among you must become like the youngest, and the leader like the servant"* (Luke 22:26).

Jesus specifically interceded for Simon Peter based on the personal target which had been placed on his back. Satan deals out his worst attacks on those he perceives are the leaders of any Spirit-led movement of God.

Those who rush to the head of the line, or campaign to have their names placed on the next best speakers' program, may not be God's chosen leaders. However, they catch Satan's eye and he puts a price on their heads and a target on their backs. It never ends well when posers persist in leading while they resist praying.

**THE PRAYER:** Jesus interceded for Peter by name. His intercession was for his faith to remain strong in the face of his failure. He knew Peter would fail. He prayed for him so his failure would not be permanent.

**THE PERMISSION:** Satan was permitted to sift and Peter was allowed to drift. This may be disturbing, but it is the truth.

**THE PROPHECY:** The sifting from Satan would lead to the drifting of Peter. Jesus knows His followers are capable of great faith and great failure. The purpose of His intercession for Peter was for him to turn to Jesus to find fresh, life-changing faith in the midst of his failure. Peter did. But Judas didn't. Big difference.

**THE PRIDE:** Peter was so full of his own sense of self-worth he missed the point of the assessment Jesus placed on the purity of his faith. His faith was in himself, not in His Savior. When Peter was about to drown in the Sea of Galilee, he cried out, *"Lord, save me!"* (Matthew 14:30). His prayer was answered. But this particular time, Peter suffered from "I" trouble and missed the

Savior's helping hand. Prideful people are prayerless, but they are never selfless: But he (Peter) said to Him, *"Lord, with You I am ready to go both to prison and to death"* (Luke 22:33).

**THE PROVISION:** Faithfulness is produced in those who refuse to drift from consistent companionship with the Savior. The Spirit fills them with this particular fruit of the character of Christ, in direct proportion to their dependence on Jesus, not their independence from Him. *"When I sent you out without money belt and bag and sandals, you did not lack anything, did you?"* (Luke 22:35).

The Cross and the Resurrection reveal the capacity of Jesus to take the impossible and turn it into the HIMpossible. Failure may appear final to Satan. The appearance of the Cross deceived the deceiver. The Father specializes in providing more faith to those who empty themselves and pray to be filled with His Spirit and His Son's faithfulness. The faithful in every generation have always done the best of things in the worst of times.

.............................

**NOTE TO SELF:** Sifting is inevitable . . . drifting is not. Being sifted by Satan doesn't mean you have to succumb to the painful process of sifting to the dangerous detour of drifting. Failure to believe in the Savior's capacity to turn the worst thing that could ever happen to you into the best thing in your life is a lack of faith. There is more faith where your first faith came from, and you must humbly pray for more to receive more. When you do, expect more faith and more sifting. To avoid falling on your face in failure, fall on your faith in Jesus.

# 16

# THE CERTAINTY

..............................

*Then Jesus raised His eyes, and said, "Father, I thank You that You have heard Me. I knew that You always hear Me; but because of the people standing around I said it, so that they may believe that You sent Me"* (John 11:41–42).

Earlier, I mentioned walking with my 93-year-old father when he spoke these simple words to me: "Peace is the blessing of believing prayer." They had nothing to do with what we had just been talking about, and they seemed to belong to a conversation he had been having with someone else. Those days, they often were.

At the last stages of Dad's life, his public ministry was no longer visible to those who knew him as a force of nature on preaching platforms and prayer conferences around the world. But on the other hand, his prayer life with the Father had never been more active and conversational.

Dad slipped in and out of conversation with others while carrying on a private conversation with the Father. He did it with such a seamless stride that it was sometimes a bit difficult to tell if he was praying or talking to me, but it was a sweet picture of his personal walk with his Savior. He seemed to be living out the words of a great old song written in 1906 (and a personal favorite of his), *Nothing Between My Soul and My Savior.*

Believing prayer has always been one of the greatest gifts Jesus has offered to His followers. This kind of prayer is deeply relational and completely conversational. It is as real as the breath in a person's lungs, and when it is repeated with the same kind of gentle regularity the answers flow, as trust in the Father grows with each fresh believing prayer.

When Jesus heard of the death of His dear friend, Lazarus, the Scripture says, *Jesus wept* (John 11:35). The passion and compassion of Jesus flowed from a heart of love for the Father and poured out on those around Him.

His tears were visible signs of His heart beating with the love of the Father and breaking over the pain that death can bring to those He loved. General Booth, founder of *The Salvation Army*, received a telegram from one of his discouraged officers, complaining of the difficulties he was facing, attempting to carry out the General's assignment. When he asked the General what to do next, Booth wired back, "Try tears."

*So Jesus, again being deeply moved within,*
*came to the tomb* (John 11:38).

Commentators debate to this day the reason for Jesus' tears. The fact remains—they were an overflow of His private and personal conversation with His Father. Perhaps they were tears of frustration. In speaking to Martha (no weak sister), and more than willing to give Jesus advice, Jesus said, *"Did I not say to you that if you believe, you will see the glory of God?"* (John 11:40).

Apparently, believing prayer was a gift Jesus had already

offered to Martha. She had a strong work ethic, but her faith was weak. Believing prayer turns your crisis over to the Father, in the name of the Son. It gives the Spirit enough elbowroom to do the heavy lifting required to reveal *"the glory of God."*

There is no great work accomplished when you figure out the least you can do, pull it off in your own strength, and then give God the glory for it.

Martha remains the poster girl for "Do it yourself Christianity." She has a huge fan base.

It gives no glory to the Father for His frantic children to pray like orphans as if the answers to their prayers depend on them, and not God. Faithless people may not be prayerless, just prideful. Don't fear asking God to do too much because people might expect you to cover the cost of what God doesn't pay when you pray.

Faithless praying weakens prayer into a stale devotional exercise, and fails to launch a great adventure. There is a huge difference between taking a walk in the park and climbing Mt. Everest. Believing prayer is worth the risk of failure—your view from the summit of answered prayer is spectacular.

> *No great work of God has ever been accomplished without the element of risk. Mark out the word risk and insert the word faith. They are one and the same.* —Dr. John Bisagno

The prayer life of Jesus reveals He maintained intimate, unbroken conversation with the Father, and He believed the Father heard Him when He prayed. He engaged in the former with confidence, but never took the latter for granted. He prayed, *"Father, I thank You that You have heard Me"* (John 11:41).

Before Jesus prayed in front of those standing around, He engaged in confident, believing prayer in private. He looked into the eyes of the Father, thanked Him, and reminded His followers, *"You always hear Me"* (John 11:42). Thank God, indeed!

Believing prayer is not based upon your eloquence, but upon your confidence in the Father. Jesus raised His eyes to the Father and looked with confidence into His eyes, knowing that the Father was already aware of the crisis at hand. Jesus prayed and allowed the Father to assume all the risks for answered prayer. Before He called for Lazarus to come forth from the grave, Jesus had been assured of the certainty that His prayer had been heard, and the answer secured.

Believing prayer resists the urge to panic in the face of a crisis, or to pacify prayer into the call of the mild. It places any choice, career, or crisis (large and small), into the Father's hands. Believing prayer trusts the Spirit to interpret the weakest prayer and deliver it to the Son. Jesus always gave all the glory to the Father for any answer to His intercession for those He loved. He still does.

..............................

**NOTE TO SELF:** When your tearless praying and prayerless preaching become completely acceptable behavior, they fall short of what passed for praying and preaching in the life of Jesus. Never settle for less, or expect more from the Father with the absence of either one in your life.

## TALK LESS! PRAY MORE!

# 17

# THE GLORY

..............................

*"Now My soul has become troubled; and what shall I say, 'Father, save Me from this hour'? But for this purpose I came to this hour. Father, glorify Your name"* (John 12:27–28).

On my last trip to Israel, I found myself looking forward to the day when our group would head to The Mount of Olives, overlooking the city of Jerusalem. It remains one of my favorite places because so little has changed, and without a doubt, it is a place where Jesus spent His final night in prayer. By the time Dana and I arrived, she had been dealing several days with a relentless stomach bug, and my luggage had not arrived. It never did. We were both a little worse for the wear, but praying in a place where Jesus took so much on His shoulders, put our travel woes in the proper perspective. Prayer has a way of shrinking my problems when I place them in the hands of Jesus and then step back and look at them through His eyes. Can I get a witness?

The glory of Jesus was a reflection of the Father's face. Jesus prayed and stayed in line with the will of the Father by never turning His face from the Father's eyes. His obedient life reflected the presence and pleasure of the Father.

The purpose of Jesus was not to make a name for Himself, but to make a difference by glorifying the name of His Father. By Jesus' prayer-fueled obedience, even unto death on the Cross, the Father honored His Son's name and made a difference through Him. Jesus radiated the presence of God.

> *And He is the radiance of His glory and the exact representation of His nature, and upholds all things by the word of His power. When He had made purification of sins, He sat down at the right hand of the Majesty on high* (Hebrews 1:3).

When Jesus prayed, the Father heard Him. When Jesus prayed, the Father answered Him. These two simple statements should fill any prayer warrior with fresh hope and renewed expectation that the prayers of Jesus, the Intercessor, are still being heard and answered. Believing prayer and answered prayer marked the prayer life of Jesus, and remains the hope of all who do what an old hymn says, "Tell it to Jesus!"

> *Christ Jesus is He who died, yes, rather who was raised, who is at the right hand of God, who also intercedes for us* (Romans 8:34).

Even in this arid culture's moral desert, there is little tolerance for those who hijack the sacrifice of dedicated war veterans. Parading around after pinning on unearned medals on cheap uniforms purchased at a local thrift shop is obscene. There are "Stolen Valor" laws on the books against the cowards. They should not go unpunished. But I digress.

At the height of His popularity, Jesus' celebrity status drew an eager audience looking for some time with Him. He responded, *"The hour has come for the Son of Man to be glorified . . . if anyone serves Me . . . the Father will honor him"* (John 12:23, 26).

Jesus did not fall into the trap Satan set. He tempts fools to substitute personal popularity for power in prayer. The focus of Jesus throughout His life on Earth was to remain pleasing to the Father. He did not waste His time gaining the approval of men, He invested His life in spending time in prayer with His Father. Kingdom fruit is produced by being consistently connected to the power of the Father, not by being well connected to men of power. Choose wisely.

*"And I, if I be lifted up from the earth, will*
*draw all men to Myself"* (John 12:32).

Jesus wasn't referencing a public relations campaign, but your death on a cross. Before Jesus was glorified He was crucified. This chronology should not escape your notice. Those who claim the name of Christ carry out His mission. The servant is never greater than the Master. If you expect to please the Father, you must follow the Son, take up your own cross, and die to self . . . not just once, but daily.

*"But He was saying this to indicate the kind of*
*death by which He was to die"* (John 12:33).

There is no glorification without crucifixion. If you want the speaking platform without spending time in the prayer closet, you may gain the prominence offered by the former, but you will never be connected to the power source of the latter. It is only a matter of time before the sad spectacle of another prayer-less preacher's private failure will lead to public embarrassment. The list of examples is too numerous to mention, and is impossible to update fast enough to remain current.

The prayers of Jesus reveal so much about His character and His love for the Father. His passion in prayer was the pleasure of the Father. His prayer life influenced His purpose in life. He became more concerned with a genuine revival than with His own personal survival—only believing prayer brings new life.

Jesus resisted the urge to escape the Cross to live for His own purpose. By praying, Jesus received the courage to die to His will and fulfill His Father's purpose. Believing prayer glorifies the Father's name and makes a difference in the world. When it comes to prayer, follow Jesus.

...........................

**NOTE TO SELF:** The glory of Jesus comes with a very high price. Don't run to the spotlight to command a stage in front of an adoring audience. Take pause before you take credit for drawing the crowd. You would be wise to take up your cross, follow Jesus, be filled with His Spirit, and die to self before you take glory for what Jesus did for you.

## TALK LESS! PRAY MORE!

# 18

# THE INTERCESSOR

..............................

*"Father, the hour has come; glorify Your Son, that the Son may glorify You, even as You gave Him authority over all flesh, that to all whom You have given Him, He may give eternal life. This is eternal life, that they may know You, the only true God, and Jesus Christ whom You have sent"*
(John 17:1–3).

John's Gospel records 26 verses, often referred to as "The High Priestly Prayer." The Intercessor packed His prayer with power, passion, and purpose. The prayers of the Intercessor still are. Whatever the size of the crisis in your face, or the weight of a concern on your heart, just tell it to Jesus.

On a personal note, my father has always referred to this passage of Scripture as, "The True Lord's Prayer." He has always believed this prayer reveals the heart of the Intercessor like no other recorded prayer of Jesus. He may be right.

After sharing The Last Supper with His disciples, Jesus expressed an intercessory prayer for those who were gathered around the table. He didn't stop there—He widened the net to include you in the army of prayer warriors who would follow in the footsteps of the faith that would be taken by this small band of brothers.

*"I do not ask on behalf of these alone, but for those who believe in Me, through their word"* (John 17:20).

Following Jesus' death, burial, resurrection on Earth, and His ascension to Heaven, the glorified Christ took His seat at the right hand of the Father. This prayer is a brief snapshot of what the Intercessor continues to do for His followers.

*Christ Jesus is He who died, yes, rather who was raised, who is at the right hand of God, who also intercedes for us* (Romans 8:34).

The Intercessor is Jesus, seated at the right hand of the Father. He stands in the gap on behalf of His followers, and He lives to intercede for them with every breath He takes. His prayers bridge the breech between their faith in God and their doubts in themselves. Pleading the case of His followers, the Son places before the Father any request (large and small), and every enemy (big and tall), that His followers place in His hands. Prayer warriors learn to confidently trust the prompting of the Spirit to place any mundane care, the latest terrifying crisis, and the heaviest concerns of their hearts into the hands of Jesus. Their childlike confidence in believing prayer is rewarded with the peace that passes all understanding in the face of their earthly warfare in the battle against evil. (See Philippians 4:7.)

Believing prayer doesn't drop your guard—it raises your confidence in the Champion. It washes your hands of the pollution of the crisis and points you to the Intercessor as the source of the solution. Believing prayer builds your confidence in Jesus, not self-confidence. Pray and trust God to bring victory in any confrontation with your relentless enemy and intimidating circumstances. In the words of my father: "Believing prayer is the transfer of a promise of God into your problem."

Believing prayer is the key that unlocks the door to eternal life. This eternal life is not postponed until death—Jesus brings to life the promises of God with every breath of prayer taken by a weary prayer warrior.

> *This is eternal life, that they may know You, the only true God, and Jesus Christ whom You have sent* (vs. 3).

Believing prayer reveals the love of the Father for His children by maintaining their consistent, confident companionship with the Intercessor. By yielding to the gentle touch of the Spirit, the wise let go of the pollution of the battle, and take hold of the hand of the Father. Jesus intercedes for you to know the solace of the Father's love, and His solution in the middle of the conflict.

..............................

**NOTE TO SELF:** War with hell is messy business. When you focus on the enemy and not the Champion, your heart will be sickened by the gore, and your hands soiled with the grime. It is too much for you to handle. Prayer takes your eyes off of the enemy and takes your hands off of the problem. Stop waiting for the peace of eternal life to begin at the point of death. It is as close as your next breath of prayer.

# 19

# THE MISSION

..............................

*"I glorified You on the earth, having accomplished the work which You have given Me to do"* (John 17:4).

One of my favorite coffee mugs bears a background image of a white-bearded Moses coming down the mountain carrying two huge stone tablets, one under each arm. In the foreground, the words of one man speaking to another are inserted and framed in the iconic comic strip bubble that says, "Oh, no! Not another mission statement." Can I get a witness?

Jesus prayed and stayed on task. The mission of His life was not to make a name for Himself, but to make a difference in the world by glorifying the Father. In His High Priestly Prayer, Jesus revealed the result of a lifetime of praying and staying on mission. He stated He had finished the work the Father had given Him to do on the Earth. What a powerful statement!

Prayerful people stay on mission by glorifying the Father. Prayerless people are prideful people who use the Father's name to make a name for themselves. In doing so, they stray from the mission—self-glorification is one of the most common forms of idolatry.

The mission of prayer is to glorify the Father. It is not accomplished by doing something for Him, or giving Him information, but in spending time with Him. The Father chooses to spend time with His children. When His children fail to pray, they fail to honor the Father.

*Though we cannot by our prayers give God*
*any information, we must by our prayers give*
*him honour.* —Matthew Henry

Going on a mission trip is often confused with being on mission. Prolific photo ops with unreached people groups are no substitute for personal participation in private prayer sessions with the Father. Taking a trip once a year may increase a poser's frequent flyer miles, but it will not make up for the precious sense of direction found in spending time in the Father's presence.

When frantic Martha raced into the presence of Jesus, she was exasperated with her sister, Mary for not helping her prepare a meal for the disciples. Surprisingly, Jesus rebuked her, and commended Mary:

*"But only one thing is necessary, for Mary*
*has chosen the good part, which shall not be*
*taken away from her"* (Luke 10:42).

Praying in the Spirit keeps you from straying from the presence of the Intercessor and the mission of the Father. Often life is inundated with unexpected crises or unappreciated divine appointments ranging from the mundane to the insane. Childish and prayerless posers take on the impossible and proudly pout: "I do it myself!" But at the first prompting of the Spirit, the heart of a childlike prayer warrior softly sings, "Tell it to Jesus."

*THE WESTMINSTER SHORTER CATECHISM of 1646:*

*Q: What is the chief end of man?*

*A: Man's chief end is to glorify God,
and to enjoy him forever.*

The prayer life of Jesus glorified the Father and gave Him great joy. His priority on praying and staying on mission should inspire you to prayerfully begin each day, face any crisis, take every breath, and overcome each hurdle in the presence of the Father. Praying led Jesus to glorify the Father . . . you should do no less.

The mission is to glorify the Father on the Earth, not to spend time giving God instructions on how to improve what He created, or complaining to Him about what He has allowed to take place on the Earth. Praying improves your capacity to see God at work and make the best, even in the worst of times.

Prayer empowers you to endure trials, pass tests, shed tears, and celebrate triumphs the way Jesus did. Jesus did not run around in panic, taking His Father's name in vain while trying to figure out what to do next. He faced whatever the enemy or life brought to Him, by placing it before the Father in prayer.

You stand next to the Champion—call out His name. Your dependence on the Son's name brings glory to the Father's name. In praying, you will receive the Father's direction, protection, and correction to carry out the mission.

Jesus was known for praying, not straying. The Father's

children honor Him by running to Him with anything that breaks their hearts or crosses their minds. They do not fear, when they sense the Father is near. Nothing glorifies Him more than praying children.

*It is a wonder what God can do with a broken heart,*
*if He gets all the pieces.* —Samuel Chadwick

...............................

**NOTE TO SELF:** When it comes to prayer, frantically working to accomplish your own mission steals your joy of being on task to accomplish the mission. Praying in the Spirit will draw you to the Father in the name of Jesus and keep you from straying from the mission. Your mission, should you agree to accept it, is impossible without prayer. Increasing your worries without increasing your praying reveals the "To Do List" of a fool. Prayer turns the impossible into MISSION HIMpossible.

## TALK LESS! PRAY MORE!

# 20

# THE REUNION

..............................

*"Now, Father, glorify Me together with Yourself, with the glory which I had with You before the world was"* (John 17:5).

A bit of nostalgia can cause people to return for a high school reunion, and the encounter can be closely related to fits of amnesia. People tend to forget the way things really were, and when they see people the way they really are, it can be a bittersweet experience.

Still, one of the sweetest reunions I have ever witnessed took place between my dad, Don Miller, and New Testament Professor, Dr. Jack McGorman. The occasion was the dedication of the McGorman Chapel and the Don and Libby Miller Prayer Room at Southwestern Baptist Theological Seminary in Fort Worth, Texas. When these two old wars horses saw each other, Dr. McGorman shouted, "Don, didn't we have a great revival meeting when you had me preach at your church?" This had only taken place 60 years earlier.

Dad beamed, and they both embraced one another, recalling and reliving their first charge up the hill. It was a sacred moment.

This verse is breathtaking in scope and substance, revealing the private, personal prayer life of the Lord, Jesus. The heartbeat of His prayer expressed His deep and abiding love for the Father, and His longing for the reunion with Him.

In one sense, the Son and the Father can never be separated from one another. They, along with the Spirit, are always together because they are the same Person. In a human sense, Jesus accepted His limitations, but longed to return to the kind of intimate relationship He once had with the Father before the world was created.

Even with all the power and authority given to Him on the Earth, these proved to be no substitute for the reunion He longed to have with the Father. Jesus came to the Earth out of obedience to the will of the Father. Personal, private prayer kept Him aligned with the Father's will, and kept His heart softened to obey Him even to the point of death. Thank You, Jesus.

*But we do see Him who was made for a little while lower than the angels, namely, Jesus, because of the suffering of death crowned with glory and honor, so that by the grace of God He might taste death for everyone* (Hebrews 2:9).

While on Earth completing the mission, Jesus utilized prayer in His intense battle against evil. To be clear, He also seized hold of prayer to maintain His personal intimacy with the Father.

Jesus was there when the world was created, and as beautiful as the creation was, the Earth held no chains on his body or charms over His heart. It paled in significance to His love for the Father and His home in Heaven.

Jesus longed to be "together" with the Father. This one word in verse 5 describes the very essence of prayer, and reveals the core value of Christianity. Faith in the Son is not a religion. He leads those who believe in Him, and bear His name, to an intimate relationship with the Father. Jesus offers no other expression of genuine faith. His followers should express nothing less.

The word "together" is a translation of the Greek preposition, "para." It is often transliterated in the English language to express very familiar terms such as parallel tracks or the teaching of parables. Each concept is a picture of a side-by-side relationship. A train is derailed if one of the tracks is not properly aligned with the other. A teaching is clarified by placing it alongside another well-known experience or widely held belief. This exhausts my personal knowledge of Greek prepositions. But I digress.

Following Jesus leads to a powerful, parallel prayer life marked by consistent companionship with the Father. Anything less than intensity for the mission and intimacy with the Father is an indication that the prayer life of the follower is out of alignment. Jesus prayed for God's will to be done in His own life. In parallel fashion, we should pray for the Fathers direction, protection, and correction in our lives.

When Jesus prayed, He hungered for the reunion with the Father. There was nothing on Earth that could satisfy the deepest longing of His heart. His obedience on Earth was His pathway to His home in Heaven, and His prelude to honor from the Father. Obedience to the Father is not only a good idea—it is God's idea. Pray and obey.

*The first purpose of prayer is to know God.* —Charles L. Allen

Praying leads to knowing the Father and obeying His will.

When you delay to obey, you will begin to stray from the Father. Jesus prayed, obeyed, and longed for the reunion. Follow Jesus' lead to receive intensity for the battle and restoration of intimacy with the Father.

..............................

**NOTE TO SELF:** Intensity and intimacy are two sides of a healthy prayer life. Prayer was forged in Heaven in the heart of the Father. Prayer was God's idea, long before you looked upon it as a good idea. Like two sides of the same coin, intensity and intimacy go together, Jesus exhibited both. You should too. Loving what you do without spending time with the Father will turn your passion into a possession. Praying reminds you to be a steward, not an owner, of what the Father has given you. Remember two things: You will never rise above your prayer life, and the best is yet to come.

## TALK LESS! PRAY MORE!

# 21

# THE MANIFEST

..............................

*"I have manifested Your name to the men whom You*
*gave Me out of the world; they were Yours and You gave*
*them to Me, and they have kept Your word. Now they*
*have come to know that everything You have given Me is*
*from You; for the words which You gave Me I have given*
*to them; and they received them and truly understood*
*that I came forth from You, and they believed that You*
*sent Me. I ask on their behalf; I do not ask on behalf of*
*the world, but of those whom You have given Me; for*
*they are Yours; and all things that are Mine are Yours,*
*and Yours are Mine; and I have been glorified in them.*
*I am no longer in the world; and yet they themselves are*
*in the world, and I come to You. Holy Father, keep them*
*in Your name, the name which You have given Me, that*
*they may be one even as We are"* (John 17:6–11).

Captains of cargo ships carry a manifest, a record detailing the
freight being carried on board. Those who insure the ship require
a clear documentation of the contents of the vessel. Those who

unload the freight check the manifest to determine if all the valuable cargo listed arrived safely to its port of destination.

In 1974 I shipped all my earthly belongings from Tanzania to Texas. I packed them in a wooden crate, put them in the back of a Land Rover truck, and hauled them to the port city of Dar es Salaam. From there they were recorded on the ship's manifest. I was given a copy of the paperwork, and told to go to Texas and wait. I was pretty sure I would never see them again. When my belongings arrived three months later in the port of Houston, Texas, they were unloaded, and then sent by truck to my home in Fort Worth. Their arrival was close to a modern day miracle.

Jesus prayed to the Father and stated, *"I have manifested Your name to the men You gave Me out of the world"* (vs. 6a).

When Jesus manifested the name of God to the men of God, He revealed the contents of His character and the Father as the source of creation and owner of all things. He knew the Father had set aside the men who would become His disciples. The manifest presence of Jesus is the real miracle.

Prior to Jesus calling the twelve disciples, He spent all night in prayer seeking His Father's wisdom and will concerning the men He would call to join Him in ministry. Throughout His life on Earth, Jesus prayed for His disciples to stay the course. Seated by the Father in Heaven, Jesus continues to intercede for you today to do the same.

*Therefore He is able also to save forever those who draw near to God through Him, since He always lives to make intercession for them* (Hebrews 7:25).

The men Jesus called to be His disciples shared at least six distinctive characteristics:

1. They belonged to God. [*"They were Yours"* (vs. 6a).]
2. They were gifts from God. [*"You gave them to Me"* (vs. 6b).]
3. They kept God's word. [*"They have kept Your word"* (vs. 6c).]
4. They knew God was the source. [*"They have come to know that everything You have given Me is from You"* (vs. 7a).]
5. They received instruction from Jesus. [*"The words which You gave Me . . . they received"* (vs. 8a).]
6. They trusted in Jesus. [*"Believed that You sent Me"* (vs. 8b).]

Jesus was not content with calling the men to come alongside of Him on the Earth—He was intent upon interceding for them. He prayed for them to be holy and separated from the world, while remaining in the world.

> *"I ask on their behalf; I do not ask on behalf of the world, but of those whom You have given Me; for they are Yours; and all things that are Mine are Yours, and Yours are Mine; and I have been glorified in them. I am no longer in the world; and yet they themselves are in the world, and I come to You"* (vs. 9–11).

Jesus is the Intercessor. He has always prayed for His disciples, but now His prayers are even more intimate and intense as He is seated at the right hand of the Father.

*For Christ did not enter a holy place made with hands,*
*a mere copy of the true one, but into heaven itself, now*
*to appear on the presence of God for us* (Hebrews 9:24).

Changing the name on *The Titanic* would not have saved it from sinking. The name of this infamous ship reflected the pride and arrogance of the owners. When those responsible for guiding the ship became more intent on gaining speed than arriving safely at their destination, disaster struck in the form of an iceberg. Those who claim the name of Christ but rebel against His authority over their lives may increase their intensity for the work of the Lord, but they will never know intimacy with the Lord of the work.

Jesus prayed that His disciples would keep themselves close to the Father's name. This required them to remain faithful children, bringing honor and glory to Him by their unity.

*"Holy Father, keep them in Your name, the*
*name which You have given Me, that they*
*may be one even as We are"* (vs. 17:11b).

The Father is not honored by disunity. When His children fight amongst themselves, they invite His correction and discipline. Jesus the Intercessor prayed then, and intercedes now, for you, His disciple, to be marked by unity not enmity and to manifest the Father's name in the lives of others. By drawing His disciples closer to Himself, Jesus releases the Father's love through them. Being filled with the Spirit of Jesus releases the love of the Father through the lives of Christ followers. When Jesus manifested the Father's name, He revealed and released His Father's love through His disciples.

..................................

**NOTE TO SELF:** The Father's love flows through you when you are filled with the Spirit. Prayer warriors who bear the Father's name are not only recipients of His love in the world; they are reflectors of it to the world. You manifest the content of His character in your life when you pray more for others than you do for yourself. Jesus manifested the Father's name and interceded for His children. You should do the same.

*As He is, so also are we in this world* (1 John 4:17b).

## TALK LESS! PRAY MORE!

## IT IS A WONDER WHAT GOD CAN DO WITH A BROKEN HEART, IF HE GETS ALL THE PIECES.

SAMUEL CHADWICK

# 22

# THE JOY

..............................

*"But now I come to You; and these things I speak in the world so that they may have My joy made full in themselves. I have given them Your word; and the world has hated them, because they are not of the world, even as I am not of the world. I do not ask You to take them out of the world, but to keep them from the evil one"* (John 17:13–15).

A few years ago I stood on "The Strip" in Las Vegas and was hit with the full sensory overload and the ultimate expression of what the world has chosen as their substitute for joy. With all the technology known to mankind, huge multistoried screens flashed gaudy and bawdy invitations to the latest and greatest sources of entertainment in the city. Entertainment is the world's substitute for joy. Like salt water, entertainment appears to have the capacity to satisfy the need for joy, but it only creates a raging thirst for more.

Jesus prayed for His disciples to be full of His joy. Those who choose to be full of themselves will never know the fullness of the joy of Jesus in themselves.

Joy is a confidence and a calm which fills the heart of a believer with gladness that spills out of them and onto others, even in the midst of the chaos and confusion of the world. To the world, this gladness looks like madness. To the Father, this calmness is a sign of His children's faithfulness. They trust in His Word and His presence to see them through the storms of life, come what may.

> *"I have given them Your word; and the world has hated them, because they are not of the world, even as I am not of the world"* (vs.14).

The disciples trusted in God's Word and shared the same citizenship with their Savior. They were living in the world that made less and less sense to them because it was no longer their home. Their homing beacon had been changed by the faith that came to them by hearing the Word of God and embracing fellowship with His Son.

> *"I do not ask You to take them out of the world, but to keep them from the evil one"* (vs. 15).

Jesus did not pray for His disciples to escape from the evil of the world but to be protected from the evil one in it. Satan is a liar, and his aim in life is to steal, kill, and destroy. He steals the joy of every believer who buys into his lies—and he lies about the meaning, and questions the authority of the Word of God. He destroys the prayer life of believers because he knows this is their source of strength.

*The one concern of the Devil is to keep the saints from praying. He fears nothing from prayerless studies, prayerless work, prayerless religion. He laughs at our toil, mocks at our wisdom, but trembles when we pray.* —Samuel Chadwick

The joy of the Christian life is not a by-product of worldly entertainment but a result of the filling of the Spirit of Christ. Entertainment has become the world's substitute for joy, but drinking from the world of entertainment never satisfies a raging thirst for joy.

Sensual, sarcastic, and shocking entertainment must continually push the edge of the envelope of decency because what once tickled a sense of humor, inevitably wears thin. The more the same punch line is used to get a laugh out of the audience, the less power it has. Comedians are often the most neurotic and joyless of people. They live for the approval of a fickle audience and become prisoners of their own success, trapped in the desert of encore anxiety. When the laughter dies, their lives have little meaning.

Joy, on the other hand, is the capacity to rise above trials, tests, and tears with a triumphal spirit. Joy does not come from tapping into a continuous stream of entertainment—the source of joy is the Spirit of Christ. Believers who yield their lives to His presence will produce His fruit, the character of Christ.

*But the fruit of the Spirit is love, joy, peace, patience, kindness, goodness, faithfulness, gentleness, self-control (Galatians 5:22–23).*

Jesus interceded for His disciples to be filled with His joy, not a man-made imitation marked by slaphappy giddiness. Love is the driving force behind the joy of Jesus. Knowing the love of the Father brings confidence and raises the level of calm in the midst of the storm. The Spirit releases joy into the heart of the believer whether they are suffocated by the mundane or overwhelmed by the insane crises of life.

Though the storm rages on, it is possible for joy to fill a wave-tossed disciple. This kind of joy comes at the point of total dependence upon, and absolute surrender to the One who holds the whole world in His hands. Joy-filled disciples don't abandon the ship, they surrender themselves to the Captain.

*When a train goes through a tunnel and it gets dark,*
*you don't throw away the ticket and jump off. You*
*sit still and trust the engineer.* —Corrie Ten Boom

Joy faces every trial, every test, and every triumph with the same kind of confidence. The Spirit's still small voice is heard within the deepest recesses of the believer's heart saying softly, "This too will pass."

Joy is an overflow, it is not just an outward expression of an inward feeling. Joy is an overflow of a filling, not a feeling. The filling of the Spirit cannot be contained or hidden by those who are filled with the character of Christ.

..............................

**NOTE TO SELF:** Your gladness may appear to be madness, but joy is calmness not madness. Praying reduces your urge to panic in the face of an enduring crisis or a cantankerous person. Your joy reflects the glory of the Father by looking into His Son's eyes in the midst of the storm. Refuse to panic until Jesus does. Like the old song, *Turn Your Eyes Upon Jesus,* says:

*Turn your eyes upon Jesus,*
*Look full in His wonderful face,*
*And the things of earth will grow strangely dim,*
*In the light of His glory and grace.*
(Helen H. Lemmel)

## TALK LESS! PRAY MORE!

# 23

# THE TRUTH

..............................

*"Sanctify them in the truth; Your word is truth. As You sent Me into the world, I also have sent them into the world. For their sakes I sanctify Myself, that they themselves also may be sanctified in truth. I do not ask on behalf of these alone, but for those also who believe in Me through their word; that they may all be one, even as You Father are in Me and I in You, that they also may be in Us, so that the world may believe that You sent Me"* (John 17:17–21).

Jesus prayed that His disciples would be kept from the evil one by being directed, protected, corrected, and saturated with the truth. The word "sanctify" describes a personal, perpetual process of consistent companionship with Jesus which allows His Spirit to exercise the freedom to convict the world of sin, and to conform believers to the image of their Savior and Lord.

Salvation is an event that can be marked on a calendar and celebrated with great joy. Sanctification is the process of dying to self. It begins with salvation, but it continues with every breath a believer takes. It is expressed by every word of truth a believer hears and obeys from the Word of God.

During my first pastorate, I sought the counsel of an older minister. A recent fire had wiped out all the work I led the church to do on a new youth building, and I was exhausted. He listened and then outlined my life in three columns on a white board. He wrote on it, "Your Call to Ministry, Your Church, Your Walk with God." He then erased the first two and asked, Which one do you think is most important? It was not a trick question, and I was not amused. He then said:

*Your walk with God is the next 20 seconds.*

I can't remember his name, but I won't forget what he said. It put the truth in perspective. If I wasn't serious about walking with God with the breath that was in my lungs, I was lying to myself. That's the truth.

Your walk with Jesus begins the moment you take your first step of obedience. The early disciples obeyed when they heard Jesus say, *"Follow Me"* (Matthew 4:19).

As His words grew more difficult to hear, other followers left Jesus, but these men stayed and obeyed.

> *As a result of this many of His disciples withdrew and were not walking with Him anymore. So Jesus said to the twelve, "You do not want to go away also, do you?" Simon Peter answered Him, "Lord, to whom shall we go? You have words of eternal life"* (John 6:66–68).

Salvation takes place on the day you identify personally with the death of Jesus on the Cross for your sin. Sanctification takes place as you daily yield your way, admit your sin, and bend your will to the yoke of Jesus. The old camp song says it all, "Wherever He leads, I'll go."

Salvation and sanctification are inseparable expressions of a genuine relationship with Jesus. Those who claim to embrace Jesus as Savior, but have no passion to obey Him as Lord, are only posing for a "selfie." They try to include Jesus as a once in a lifetime photo op but they have no desire to walk with Him daily. They settle for being a poser with Jesus without ever being a follower of Jesus. This is neither salvation nor sanctification.

Salvation is the result of the first step of obedience but sanctification is the result of daily steps of obedience. Jesus expected His disciples then, and now, to accept Him as their crucified Savior and to allow His Spirit to transform them into sanctified followers of His Lordship. He prayed for no less.

Sanctify is rich in meaning and carries the weight of many words to describe it clearly. It means: To set apart, to make holy, to hallow, to dedicate, to consecrate, and to purify. Anyone connected with God carries the stamp of His sacred character upon their inward souls, and on their outward behavior. When it comes to the fruit of the Spirit, the apple never falls far from the tree.

Jesus prayed for His disciples to be sanctified in the truth of God's Word. Praying and obeying the Word of God will guide any believer away from the pollution of the world and towards the Father's solution for the world, His Son, Jesus Christ.

> *"I am the way, and the truth, and the life; no one comes to the Father but through Me"* (John 14:6).

Self-gratification and self-glorification are the twin towers of self-satisfaction. Sanctification is marked by self-denial and absolute surrender to Holy God and His Son's Lordship. The citizens of the Kingdom take on the character of the King by praying for Him to finish in the yoke what He began in them at the Cross.

*Before we can pray, "Lord, Thy Kingdom come," we must be willing to pray, "My Kingdom go."* —Alan Redpath

..................................

**NOTE TO SELF:** What you do with your next breath determines the direction, protection, and correction of your life. Consider the importance of the prayer of Jesus. He places a very high priority upon the sanctification of His disciples and those who would believe in Him through their word. Don't try to clean the fish before you catch them. The world is a polluted place, but that is where the fish are found. Catching precedes the cleaning of the fish. Cleaning never leads to catching fish. Trying to clean fish before you catch them only frustrates you and annoys the fish. Stop it.

## TALK LESS! PRAY MORE!

# 24

# THE POINT

..............................

*"I do not ask on behalf of these alone, but for those
also who believe in Me through their word; that they
may all be one; even as You, Father, are in Me and I
in You, that they also may be in Us, so that the world
may believe that You sent Me"* (John 17:20–21).

The point of the prayer of Jesus is for believers in Him, then and
now, to *"all be one"* (vs. 21). There is a difference between closeness and oneness. The dilemma of many people posing as believers is that they are so close, but yet so far away. There is little hope
found in the proverbial statement, "Close, but no cigar."

The union of a cat and a dog can take place by tying their tails
together. This form of closeness occurs by the union of bod-
ies, without any oneness of heart. Jesus did not pray for union
among disagreeing disciples but for oneness. He prayed, *"even
as You, Father, are in Me and I in You"* (vs. 21).

*Single-hearted* was the name of the Single Adult ministry
my wife, Dana, and I conducted in Houston, Texas in the early
1980s. Our mission was to develop servants in the local Church

marked by "sincerity and unity of purpose." Many of them accepted the challenge to raise their purpose in life above the fulfillment of their own personal preferences, and found great joy in being one with the Father and with other believers.

The local Church still remains the best lab for developing the kind of oneness that is produced by Spirit-filled believers. The Apostle Paul described the vital sign of oneness as fullness of the Spirit and marked by mutual submission between believers.

*And be subject to one another in*
*the fear of Christ* (Ephesians 5:21).

Lone Ranger Christianity may succeed in removing oneself from the company of the cantankerous—there is great relief in escaping the irritation that comes from the constant chafing of being in close quarters with calloused Christians.

But still, Jesus prayed for His disciples to have a oneness in Him and in the Father. This kind of oneness was meant to create compassion in the heart of each believer and improve the capacity of the body of believers to coordinate and cooperate with one another.

*It is easy to be an angel as long as no one ruffles*
*your feathers.* —Unknown Author

The U.S. Army once called upon potential recruits to sign up and be "The Army of One." Jesus prayed then, and intercedes now, for His disciples to become "The Army of Oneness." Big difference. John's Gospel reveals that Jesus prayed for His disciples and for those who believed in their word, *"that they also may be in Us"* (vs. 21).

Words mean things. Believing words *about* Jesus, and being *in* Jesus are two very different things. Talking *about* marriage and *being* married are not the same thing.

One of the earliest pieces of marriage advice I recall is the statement, "You will have to be married to realize how selfish you really are." Though I didn't believe it then, truer words have never been spoken.

Marriage remains the best field for producing the fruit of oneness Jesus prayed for His disciples to have in Him and in the Father. It is described as a one-flesh relationship in Mark 10:8. This does not refer merely to occasional sexual union. It describes the perpetual and mutual submission produced by the fullness of the Spirit (see Ephesians 5:21).

Believing in Jesus leads to being in the Father. Anything less than this kind of personal intimacy is not oneness. Personal preference and claiming rights are out of bounds for those who are *"in Us"* (vs. 21).

When an individual athlete is in "the zone," it describes that rare moment when personal talent and diligent training come together in the arena of competition, revealed for all to see. As beautiful as this is, it is nothing compared to the sight of a team of individuals merging into a coordinated body and cooperating together to achieve a common goal.

As coaches often say, "There is no 'I' in TEAM." There is also no "I" in PRAY. When Jesus prayed for His disciples (and when He prays for them now) He invited them to join His team, not to be a star of their own.

..................................

**NOTE TO SELF:** In prayer, Jesus met with the Father early in the day, throughout the day, and at times, all night long, to conform His will to the Father's will. He prayed long enough to be in Him, not just to be with Him. You should pray until you are in the Father, single-hearted, marked by sincerity, and the unity of His purpose. The oneness Jesus describes between Himself and His Father is offered to you. Jesus found it in praying to the Father. You should not expect to find it any other way.

## TALK LESS! PRAY MORE!

BELIEVING PRAYER IS THE
TRANSFER OF A PROMISE OF
GOD INTO YOUR PROBLEM.

DON MILLER

# 25

# THE UNITY

....................................

*"The glory which You have given Me I have given to them, that they may be one, just as We are one; I in them and You in Me, that they may be perfected in unity, so that the world may know that You sent Me, and loved them, even as You have loved Me"* (John 17:22–23).

American History reveals that during December of 1941, rabid isolationists merged with robust interventionists after the Japanese bombed Pearl Harbor and Germany declared war on the United States. This did not mean that isolationists were united in their love for interventionists. It just meant they hated The Axis powers more. Real unity is driven by love, not hate.

The prayer of Jesus reveals a present glory and a future glory. There is an unmistakable reflection of the glory of God upon the lives of believers who have the person of Jesus dwelling within them. There is also a hope in His prayer that the best is yet to come. Believers need a firm grip on both, the here and now, and the sweet by and by.

Jesus prays for a oneness that exists between believers marked by the very same oneness that exists between the Father and the Son. This oneness is a unity initiated by seekers taking the tiniest step of faith towards Jesus and embracing Him as their personal Lord and Savior.

This unity is completed, or perfected, in seekers turned believers, by the process of yielding breath-by-breath, day-by-day, and prayer-by-prayer, to the gentle promptings of the Spirit of Christ. The greatest evidence the world will ever see of the work of the Spirit is not a feeling in a person, but a filling of a believer that leads to a changed life. The turnaround is a change of heart, mind, and direction. This change is not a result of a feeling, but a filling of the Spirit—the world needs living proof.

> *"Perfected in unity, so that the world may know that You sent Me, and loved them, even as You have loved Me"* (vs. 23).

Unity is more than an undesirable union between two independent thinking people. Forcing people to be in close proximity to those they have no power to love only leads to independent lecture series or open warfare. Unity is reflected by the mutual submission between two believers prompted by complete submission to the love and the Lordship of Christ. Those who embrace the labor of God without the love of Christ generate sweat equity without bearing sweet fruit. Loveless labor turns the Church into a sweatshop reeking of perspiring flesh, not a farmer's market of sweet smelling fruit.

*The enemy of my enemy is my friend.* —Arab Proverb

For those who suffer from poor self-esteem and for those

who esteem themselves more highly than they should, Jesus stated that the Father *"loved them"* (vs. 23). For those trapped in self-pity or for those elevated by their self-made status, Jesus declared the Father's love is an "in spite of " love, not a "because of " love (see John 3:16). The love of the Father prompted Him to send His Son to those who had no hope of being made right by their own effort. Those with poor self-esteem or high self-esteem have one thing in common, S.E.L.F. (Selfish Egos Living Freely). Self has to die before the new birth takes place and the perfection of unity begins.

*But God demonstrates His own love toward us, in that while we were yet sinners, Christ died for us* (Romans 5:8).

Before He went to the Cross, Jesus prayed to conform His will to the Father's will—to share His love with those who needed it the most but didn't deserve it in the least. When He died on the Cross, Jesus stated: *"It is finished!"* (John 19:30).

What Jesus finished on the Cross He intends to perfect in you. Follow His lead and die daily. Prayer releases in the lives of believers the love of the Father. His love is more than a feeling—it is the filling of His Spirit which leads to unity among His children.

...........................

**NOTE TO SELF:** Laboring with someone you can't stand, to destroy an enemy both of you hate, is not a labor of love. Even honest or Bible-based labor, accomplished with effectiveness and efficiency, does not make it a labor of love. Hating Satan without loving your neighbor sheds more heat than light. Don't settle for perspiration without illumination.

# 26

# THE DESIRE

..............................

*"Father, I desire that they also, whom You have given Me, be with Me where I am, so that they may see My glory which You have given Me, for You loved Me before the foundation of the world"* (John 17:24).

One day a farmer and his wife were driving their old truck to town. The smooth bench seat separated them, as he held the steering wheel and she leaned against the armrest of the passenger side door. The farmer's wife spoke in a wistful tone, "We don't sit together like we used to." The farmer responded, "I ain't moved."

The prayer of Jesus reveals the deepest desire of the Savior was for His followers to *"be with Me where I am"* (vs. 24). Jesus proclaimed Himself as *"I AM"* seven times in the Gospel of John.

With each of these seven declarations, Jesus gave His disciples a glimpse into His divine nature and His presence in the present tense. He did not say: "I was" or "I will be." He declared: *"I AM."* There is nothing in the world like knowing the presence of Jesus in the present tense.

*I AM . . .*
- *The Bread* (John 6:35)
- *The Light* (John 8:12)
- *The Door* (John 10:7)
- *The Good Shepherd* (John 10:11)
- *The Resurrection and The Life* (John 11:25)
- *The Way, The Truth, and The Life* (John 14:6)
- *The Vine* (John 15:5)

Each statement is a clear identification of His oneness and unity with the Father.

Public prayer is a poor substitute for private prayer, and the former often reveals the need for more of the latter. When someone prays, "Lord, be with us," they need to be reminded of Biblical truth.

> *"Be strong and courageous. Do not be afraid or terrified because of them, for the LORD your God goes with you; he will never leave you nor forsake you"* (Deuteronomy 31:6 NIV).

> *"Never will I leave you; never will I forsake you"* (Hebrews 13:5 NIV).

Praying, "Lord, be with us," often reveals an expectation for the Father to move towards rebellious children. The Father has an expectation for His children to return and run toward Him. God is responsive to the prayers of His children, but He is looking for them to come to Him with a broken heart, not just their broken toys.

Too many times rebellious children want God to fix what their own hands have broken, without a change of heart. This is not prayer. It is wistful thinking.

> *Two things break God's heart:*
> *Rebellion and repentance.* —Don Miller

The Apostle James recognized this change of heart and the responsiveness of God, and challenged the early Church in James 4:8 to: *Draw near to God and He will draw near to you.*

King David knew the joy of coming face-to-face with God in the midst of his tears and brokenness in Psalm 88:2: *Incline Your ear to my cry!*

Perhaps there is no greater personal victory in prayer than that moment in time, in the middle of a personal *valley of the shadow of death*, that a broken-hearted prayer warrior comes to the same realization as King David and says, *You are with me* (Psalm 23:4).

It is not much of a stretch of faith to believe the prayer of Jesus was heard and answered by the Father. His prayers always have been, and they still are—He is praying in the present tense for His disciples to be with Him.

Prayer is still the way the followers of Jesus gain an audience with the Father and are granted the desires of their heart through the intercession of the Son.

> *Delight yourself in the LORD; And He will give*
> *you the desires of your heart* (Psalm 37:4).

..............................

**NOTE TO SELF:** Jesus desires for you to be with Him. It is not only your future hope in Heaven—He offers His presence in the present tense on Earth. If the Father's love seems far away, run to Jesus. If God seems far away, guess who moved? Jesus prayed for His followers to be with Him—the next question is: Are you with Him?

## TALK LESS! PRAY MORE!

THOUGH WE CANNOT BY
OUR PRAYERS GIVE GOD ANY
INFORMATION, WE MUST BY OUR
PRAYERS GIVE HIM HONOUR.

MATTHEW HENRY

# 27

# THE RIGHTEOUS

..............................

*"O righteous Father, although the world has not known You, yet I have known You; and these have known that You sent Me; and I have made Your name known to them, and will make it known, so that the love with which You have loved Me may be in them, and I in them"* (John 17:25–26).

The prayer of Jesus to His righteous Father reveals the source of righteous children. Being made right with the Father begins with confession of one's personal separation from Him, and it leads to identification with the death of His Son. Jesus is the only way to be declared right by Him.

*"I am the way, and the truth, and the life; no one comes to the Father but through Me"* (John 14:6).

Jesus prayed for His disciples to be filled with the Father's love. The righteous Father has no fellowship with rebellious children, only righteous children. Those who are righteous have been justified, made right in His eyes, by identifying with the death of His Son on the Cross. This is justification, and it is not a matter of education, but transformation.

Knowing about the death of Jesus and being transformed by His death are not the same thing.

There is a huge difference between a farmer's market and a machine shop. Both require a great deal of effort, but each has a unique aroma. When I was a small boy, one of my favorite things to do was accompany my dad to the Dallas Farmer's Market. Fruit and produce from farms all over Central Texas were displayed from the back of pickups. Sunburned men and women, with calloused hands, proudly cut open cantaloupe, watermelons, peaches, and corn. The aroma of the Farmer's Market smelled like fruit. The odor of a machine shop smells like men, motors, and machinery.

Righteous children not only wear the name of the Father, they bear His fruit by sharing His love. Jesus prayed for His disciples to not only be informed about the Father's name and wear it like a phony good luck charm, but interceded for them to bear genuine fruit and to be conformed to the Father's love. He still does.

Jesus prayed for His disciples to be filled with *"the love with which You have loved Me"* (vs. 26). When Jesus is invited into the lives of His disciples, He not only places His name on His followers, He brings the Father's love into them. *"I in them"* (vs. 26) was His prayer then, and now. The Father's love is still the hope of the world. Don't offer the world your own version of imitation fruit.

*The fruit of the Spirit is love* (Galatians 5:22).

..................................

**NOTE TO SELF:** The Father's love for you was undeserved. Jesus prayed for His love to be expressed by you to those who need it the most, and deserve it the least. You are not a fruit inspector. You are a fruit bearer.

### TALK LESS! PRAY MORE!

BEWARE OF ANY WORK FOR GOD THAT CAUSES OR ALLOWS YOU TO AVOID CONCENTRATING ON HIM.

OSWALD CHAMBERS

# 28

# THE LOVE

..............................

*"And I have made Your name known to them, and will make it known, so that the love with which You loved Me may be in them, and I in them"* (John 17:26).

*"I in them."* These are the last three words of the prayer of Jesus and may contain the most profound concept ever verbalized by the Savior. It distills into three small words, simple enough for a child to read: His message, His mission, and His greatest miracle to mankind. Jesus offers to enter into His followers and reveal the Father's love for them, and through them, one life at a time.

One Wednesday night I was driving home after a long day when our youngest daughter, Allyson, asked me a question. This wasn't unusual—she was always talkative and inquisitive, and her interests were wide-ranging—often skipping across my pond like a well-thrown, smooth stone. I always enjoyed our little "talks," but they were exhausting!

That night, Allyson asked: "Can Jesus come into my heart?" I immediately went on a "Red Fox" full alert—this was the big one. Before I could answer, she framed the debate with a follow-up question: "He is so big, and I am so little. How can He get into my heart?" I gave her the best shot that I had in my gun: "When we get home, ask your mother." Thanks, Dana—you took one for the team that night.

Childlike faith doesn't debate the integrity of the kind of intimacy Jesus offers to those He loves. Childlike faith embraces Jesus and leaves the details to Him.

The Apostle Paul referred to the mystery of the Gospel in Romans 16:25. He understood it as a great secret that had been revealed. God loved the world in such a way, the angels in Heaven were stunned by the scope of His love. Repentant sinners and His rebellious children continue to be surprised by His grace. Thank God!

The greatness of God's love was completely lost on Satan. Even though he heard the truth spoken in John 3:16, his pride was unable to yield to *the way, and the truth, and the life* of John 14:6.

*"For God so loved the world, that He gave
His only begotten Son"* (John 3:16).

*"No one comes to the Father
but through Me"* (John 14:6).

The goal of the evil one is to keep people from receiving God's love. He does this by tempting them to doubt and debate God's word, delay the application, or distort the meaning of it.

The love of God is not earned—His love is received. Jesus does not offer God's love through the crystal clear knowledge of an essential doctrine or a well-documented, refined definition. Jesus offers Himself. The Father's love is discovered through an intimate, consistent companionship with Him.

When I fell in love with my beautiful wife, it was love at first sight. From that moment on, I have learned more about her, and continue to discover aspects of her that I never knew existed. Dana is like a diamond which cannot be seen in one setting or one set of circumstances. When breast cancer threw her life against a dark backdrop, the reflection of her personal love relationship with Jesus was not snuffed out. It only shone more brilliantly.

Simply put, I love her more today than the first day I met her, and the best is yet to come. The same is true with my love for Jesus. I thought I knew Him. But I am just beginning to experience the truth of, *"I in them"* (vs. 26).

This is not to say that the presence of Jesus is a feeling, but the love of the Father is a filling. Jesus offers His filling to those who yield to the Spirit.

Again, the filling is not a liquid additive, but a personal relationship that takes the place of anything or anyone else. Those who are filled are under new ownership and willingly receive the Father's direction, protection, and correction.

Praying is not a high-minded devotional exercise—it is a humble-hearted yielding to the Father's will. Follow Jesus, lean on Him, and learn to love by yielding your will the same way Jesus did—praying to the Father. When you're in need of the love of the Father, run to Jesus!

*But the fruit of the Spirit is love* (Galatians 5:22).

*"Not My will, but Yours be done"* —Jesus (Luke 22:42).

..................................

**NOTE TO SELF:** When the prayer of Jesus ends with "I in them," He is offering you a promise of His presence, come what may. Faith comes by hearing. When you hear Jesus pray this promise, take Him at His word. Today, begin to receive the love of the Father. The love of the Father that is offered through His Son cannot be fully explained—Jesus must be experienced.

### TALK LESS! PRAY MORE!

THE FIRST PURPOSE OF PRAYER
IS TO KNOW GOD.

CHARLES L. ALLEN

# 29

# THE FATHER

.................................

*"Father . . . glorify Your Son, that the*
*Son may glorify You"* (John 17:1).

The other day I asked my father, "What is the one thing you would want people to know about prayer, if it was the last thing you could share with them?" He said:

> *Follow Jesus. It just isn't any more complicated*
> *than that. Don't complicate prayer. Jesus cannot*
> *be explained. He must be experienced.*

'Nuff said.

In the prayer of Jesus, the Son addressed the Father as Holy God. When Jesus responded to His disciples' request, *"Lord, teach us to pray,"* (Luke 11:1), Jesus offered them the same gracious and intimate access to His Father. He said, *"Pray, then, in this way, 'Our Father who is in heaven'"* (Matthew 6:9).

When Jesus established the constitution of the Kingdom,

He introduced the standards for citizenship, *"poor in spirit"* (Matthew 5:3). He described those who humbled themselves (were not spiritually arrogant), rather than full of themselves.

When the arrogant disciples of Jesus needed an object lesson of this kind of humility—a childlike trust in the authority and jurisdiction of the Father—the Son reached out for the hand of a little one and said, *"Unless you are converted and become like children, you will not enter the kingdom of heaven. Whoever then humbles himself as this child, he is the greatest in the kingdom of heaven"* (Matthew 18:3–4).

The prayer of Jesus begins with Him humbling Himself in the presence of the Father, and it ends with the Son interceding before the Father for His disciples to be filled with His love. They needed to be full of Jesus, not themselves—His disciples still do. Jesus still intercedes for you to experience, *"I in them"* (John 17:23). Thank You, Jesus.

Reading about prayer, talking about prayer, singing about prayer, and preaching about prayer must lead to more praying. Anything less is a delay in intimacy with the Father. *"Unless you are converted"* (Matthew 18:3) should encourage every prayerless disciple that personal, private prayer is the way a rebellious child is able to turn their prideful and prayerless heart into a humble and prayerful heart. Two things break the Father's heart: Rebellion and repentance. Prayerful children are humble children who turn around at the slightest call of the Father and run to Him in the name of the Son, Jesus.

There is nothing like the presence of the Father. Jesus longed for the Father's presence and found His way to Him early in the day, during the day, late at night, throughout the night, in public places, and on prolonged, private retreats. Jesus saturated Himself with the Father's presence by yielding His will to the

Father's will. As His disciples, we should do no less.

..............................

**NOTE TO SELF:** When you start complicating prayer or become satisfied with being educated about prayer, you stop coming into the presence of the Father. Rebellious children start delaying and stop praying. Choose to seek His direction, protection, and correction.

### TALK LESS! PRAY MORE!

THE ONE CONCERN OF THE DEVIL IS
TO KEEP THE SAINTS FROM PRAYING.
HE FEARS NOTHING FROM PRAYERLESS
STUDIES, PRAYERLESS WORK,
PRAYERLESS RELIGION. HE LAUGHS AT
OUR TOIL, MOCKS AT OUR WISDOM,
BUT TREMBLES WHEN WE PRAY.

SAMUEL CHADWICK

# 30

# THE WHILE

..............................

*While they were eating, Jesus took some bread, and after a blessing, He broke it and gave it to the disciples, and said, "Take, eat; this is My body." And when He had taken a cup and given thanks, He gave it to them, saying, "Drink from it, all of you* (Matthew 26:26-27). (See also Mark 14:22–25, Luke 22:19–20, 1 Corinthians 11:24–25.)

As a child, one of the more difficult measurements for me to learn was the length of time expressed by a "while." On a long road trip, I would often ask, "When are we going to get there?" The most bewildering response I could ever hear from my parents was the phrase, "In a while."

It was a mind-numbing, moving target. My parents had an agenda, and they were in charge of the schedule. Pleasing me was not as important as arriving safely at the destination. Jesus has a similar purpose for my life. He is continuously preparing to teach me some of His greatest lessons while I am focused on something else.

One of the more important, and perhaps one of the most

underrated, words in the Bible may be the repeated expression translated as "while." It appears things are not always what they seem to be in the Kingdom. While an event may be scheduled, and Jesus chooses to be present, He often has an entirely different agenda in mind for the occasion.

"While" insane crises surged into Jesus' life, or mundane circumstances siphoned strength out of His life, He prayed and stayed in touch with the Father. By praying in His Spirit, Jesus empowered His followers to replace fear with faith, and make sense out of the senseless. He still does that today.

But the prayerless miss Jesus "while" trying to keep their head above water through tumultuous times. The prayerful should find fresh meaning in life, even when time stands still. They should refuse to just go through the motions. They should discover fresh faith and prayer-fueled expectancy, with every breath of prayer they take.

"While" the twelve disciples gathered to share the traditional feast of the Passover with Jesus, He gave it a whole new meaning to them. At the close of it, Jesus had a few final words for them. After all is said and done, what really matters in life is what Jesus says and does, after we have done all we think we can do.

"While" is that side of life which appears to be the worst thing that can happen. Prayer takes the time to bring the infuriating and the uninspiring seasons of life to the Father, in the name of the Son. Through prayer, fearful and faithless eyes can become adjusted to the dark, and see what the Father had in mind all along.

"While" takes place in the fiery furnaces or on the dusty shelves of life. Prayerful people should refuse to be prideful. Give the Spirit elbowroom in your life and seek the Father's direction. Humbly seek His protection in the furnace, or His correction on the shelf. Through prayer, the prideful will is yielded to the Father's will.

Prayer has a way of clearing away the fog of war and allowing a prayer warrior to see the battle is won and their lives are in the hands of the Father. From a prayerless perspective, people panic in the furnace, put down roots on the shelf, and begin to believe the end has come. But truly, the best is yet to come.

Even prayerful people can become victims of past successes and answered prayers. Don't grow comfortable on the shelf of a plateau, and succumb to the soothing lies of the evil one that it just doesn't get any better than this. Prayer brings the Father's children into His arms in the name of the Son, and He raises them above their own perspective to reveal His own view of their current crisis or their senseless circumstance. He will show you how to survive in the former and how to be revived in the latter. Through prayer, you will develop the faith to do both. I promise.

*While they were eating* (Matthew 26:26), Jesus was preparing Himself to share with His disciples that the best was yet to come. It still is. At the Last Supper, the disciples didn't see it coming. Neither did hell. Jesus still loves to surprise His followers, and amaze the world with His grace--thank You, Jesus.

...............................

**NOTE TO SELF:** Some of the Father's greatest gifts to His children are wrapped up in the scariest packaging and tied up with a thorny bow. Receive the Father's perspective and follow His directive "while" you are in the furnace or on the shelf. The Cross looked like it was the worst thing that could happen—it wasn't. Never forget. Looks can be deceiving. "While" you are in it, don't panic at the sight of it. Run to Jesus and pray your way through it.

# 31

# THE BLESSING

...........................

*After a blessing He broke it, and gave it to them,*
*and said, "Take it; this is My body"* (Mark 14:22).

Growing up, saying "The Blessing" in our family was always a mixed blessing. Mom would put the food on the table and the four of us kids knew better than to leap at it before it was blessed. If anyone got in a rush and put some food in their mouth, Dad would immediately call on that kid to say the blessing. The worst was when our family went to eat at Wyatt's Cafeteria. After we unloaded our trays, Dad would insist on saying a blessing over our food IN PUBLIC. It was never silent. It was LOUD, and it was long. I always rubbed my eyes, and acted like I didn't know what was going on. It was not my finest hour. But I digress.

The blessing of Jesus preceded His introduction of the Last Supper. It is not recorded what Jesus prayed, but the Blessing is remembered every time the Last Supper is presented. The blessing is a symbol of the body and the blood of Jesus.

Saying a blessing over a meal is one of the first signs of maturity wise parents model for their little ones to express. Children do not come into this world with an attitude of gratitude. Only foolish parents fail to cultivate the development of a spirit of thanksgiving in their selfish children.

This is not to mean a parent should abdicate the responsibility of saying "The Blessing," to their children. Many parents urge reluctant little ones in public to "Say the blessing." This should never become a cop out for those who would rather not be embarrassed by doing it themselves.

At the Last Supper, Jesus blessed the bread, broke it, gave it to "The Twelve," and identified it as His own body. Mark's Gospel account records no evidence of a discussion or a debate breaking out among "The Twelve" over the meaning of the blessing of Jesus. They heard what He had to say, did what He said to do, and *After singing a hymn, they went out to the Mount of Olives* (Mark 14:26). And then Jesus prayed all night. But the three whom Jesus called to pray with Him fell asleep. Don't be like them—follow Jesus.

This simple pattern that appears in Mark's account of the Last Supper may be the clearest outline of a genuine worship service. Those who follow it will discover the blessing in it.

"The blessing" is translated from a Greek word which is often translated into English as "eulogy." When asked to give a eulogy at a funeral, a preacher is expected to extol the virtue and the reputation of the one who has died.

This honorable task is complicated by the absence of any evidence that the person represented by the body in the casket ever obeyed anything Jesus told them to do. Those who are alive in Christ will always choose to pray and obey.

The blessing turns death into life when the followers of Jesus identify with His body on the Cross. Before He offered His body to die on the Cross, Jesus offered the Passover bread as a symbol of His body that He would place on the Cross.

Jesus offered bread that had no yeast, as a representation of His sinless life. Only the sinless body of the Son can be the acceptable substitute, received by the Father for the sins of His wicked, wayward children.

> *"For you first, God raised up His Servant and sent Him to bless you by turning every one of you from your wicked ways"* (Acts 3:26).

The blessing of new life comes to those who don't make excuses for their sin but they identify personally with the death of Jesus on the Cross. They come to the point where they agree that Jesus did this for them. Through prayer, they yield their will, agree with the Father's assessment of their behavior, and the price Jesus paid for them to be right with the Father. The blessing is still offered by Jesus and is only a prayer away. Stop making excuses.

.............................

**NOTE TO SELF:** Jesus still blesses those who follow Him. Listen to Jesus, identify with Him, and immediately obey Him. Sing a hymn, leave the room, pray to the Father, and then prepare to die by surrendering your will. Take up your cross, die on it, and do this daily.

## TALK LESS! PRAY MORE!

# 32

# THE REMEMBRANCE

..............................

*And when He had taken a cup and given thanks, He said,
"Take this and share it among yourselves; for I say to you,
I will not drink of the fruit of the vine from now on until
the kingdom of God comes." And when He had taken
some bread and given thanks, He broke it and gave it to
them, saying, "This is My body which is given for you;
do this in remembrance of Me." And in the same way He
took the cup after they had eaten, saying, "This cup which
is poured out for you is the new covenant in My blood"*
(Luke 22:17–20).

In February of 1957 while seated in the morning celebration
of The Lord's Supper at Forney Avenue Baptist Church in Dallas, Texas, the Holy Spirit began a work in my heart. I didn't
know Him by name in those days but I sensed His presence.
The childlike always do. The childish never will.

For five years I had been watching this observance in our
church. Every week I took my place in "Big Church" on the
third row, right next to my mother. As a first grader I had

learned to read, and now I could make out the big, bold letters carved into the table right in front of the pulpit, "DO THIS IN REMEMBRANCE OF ME."

As the plate of bread passed me by I did not partake. It bothered me. It had never bothered me before when Mom wouldn't allow me to participate. This time it was different.

The passing of the shallow, metal plate of square, yeast-free pellets, along with the small, glass cups filled with Welch's Grape Juice was a regular part of my religious upbringing in a Southern Baptist church. Each time the plate of bread and round trays of cups reached my row, Mom would take one of each, and then pass them on. I knew I was not allowed to take part, but I just didn't know why.

Being passed over didn't happen every week, just every few months or so. Being excluded from participating in the celebration of the Lord's Supper didn't make sense to me. I had been attending church nine months before I was even born. I attended Sunday School, Big Church, Training Union, Sunday Night Church, Royal Ambassadors, Wednesday Night Prayer Meeting, church-wide visitation on Thursday nights, VBS, and Friday night softball games in the summer. In spite of all the participation in church activities, I realized I was different from the members who partook of the bread and the juice of The Lord's Supper.

But this time I started asking questions, and I wanted answers. My questions led to a private meeting with my dad right after lunch at The Parsonage on 1426 South Fitzhugh. Sitting on the side of the bed in my parent's back bedroom of that little wooden framed house, I came face-to-face with a big decision. I recognized my sin. I was clever enough to hide my behavior from my parents, but I knew in my heart I could not hide it from God. Without even knowing the definition of sin, I was under conviction. The childlike may not be able to define sin, but they want it forgiven. The childish excuse it.

My personal sense of separation from God was simple and childlike but very real. I could no longer delay dealing with it. I had been taught, "God is love." I had sung *Jesus Loves Me*. I had head knowledge, but I lacked a forgiven heart. I was aware I was wrong in God's eyes and I desired to be right with Him.

After a quiet talk with my dad, I knelt down by his bed and prayed. I don't remember the words of the prayer—but I remember I prayed in the name of Jesus. When I got up from praying, I no longer sensed a separation from God, I sensed His pleasure with me. This childlike prayer was my first step of faith and the placing of my confidence in the name of Jesus. After 60 years . . . the journey continues and so do my prayers. Thank You, Jesus.

From Luke's account of the Last Supper, this powerful scene seems to have had little impact on "The Twelve." After saying thanks over the bread and the cup, and sharing both with His disciples, *they began to discuss among themselves . . . and there arose also a dispute among them as to which one of them was regarded to be greatest* (Luke 22:23–24).

When the contemporary church starts remembering the Cross of Jesus, they will stop dismembering one another. When believers remember where their journey began with Jesus, it brings them to the end of themselves and back to the Cross. When being greater than others becomes more important than being right with God, it is a sure sign of self-centeredness and the existence of a pressing need to be made right with God. Self-importance is a poor substitute for self-denial—Jesus values the latter, not the former.

*"And he who does not take his cross and follow after Me is not worthy of Me"* —Jesus (Matthew 10:38).

...............................

**NOTE TO SELF:** Taking up your cross and following after Jesus begins with remembering what He did for you on the Cross and thanking Him for it. You need to do this daily. Don't lean on a church celebration to remind you on a weekly or quarterly basis. Habitually whining about what you have sacrificed to follow after Jesus should remind you to get off "The Whine" and break out "The Welch's." Kick the habit.

## TALK LESS! PRAY MORE!

# 33

# THE CUP

..............................

*Then he took a cup of wine and gave thanks to God for it . . . After supper he took another cup of wine and said, "This cup is the new covenant between God and his people—an agreement confirmed with my blood, which is poured out as a sacrifice for you"* (Luke 22:17a, 20 NLT).

When I was a student at Baylor University, at the urging of one of my church history professors, I began a life-long study of "The Left Wing Reformationists." Give me a minute to explain.

My professor suggested I take a look at what happened after Martin Luther nailed his theses to the wall of the cathedral door in Germany and Zwingli cleared the religious clutter out of the churches in Switzerland.

What I discovered was pretty messy—Spiritual Awakening always is.

In the 16th century, the reading of the Word of God unleashed a wide range of activity in the religious world. In a panic search for truth, some people went off the deep end and some went off the shallow end. When honest brokers encounter the truth of Scripture for the first time in their lives, some go for broke, and some go bankrupt. Pretty messy, indeed.

Luther led the Germans and Zwingli led the Swiss as they fought it out among themselves along the lines of The Lord's Supper. Both reformers couldn't bring themselves to agree with the Roman Catholics. As they read the Scripture, they chose a more symbolic meaning of The Supper.

The two words I recall jumping out at me in this study were "mere symbolism." As 16th century reformers studied the words of Jesus, they struggled to keep the meaning of His words to His disciples from being elevated to something Jesus never intended to say. They also didn't want the Savior's words being deteriorated into "mere symbolism." For 21st century Christians, the dangers of both extremes still exist.

In the Upper Room, Jesus described the contents of the cup as His blood—which was a symbol. When Jesus poured out His blood on the Cross He did not merely offer a symbol—He made a real sacrifice. Big difference.

The Old Testament encouraged fathers to lead their families as heads of their households to worship at the temple. On the Day of Atonement they were told to bring a sacrifice and offer it on behalf of their family. In doing so, they were to bring the best they had to offer and identify with the death of the animal, in order to be made right with God.

As the sacrificial animal was being prepared for death, the father would place his hands on the head of the animal. In this way, the sins of the fathers and their families would be symbolically transferred. At the shedding of the animal's death the sins would be atoned for in the eyes of God, but the blood of the animal was only one part of the sacrifice. The identification with the death of the animal was the father's key part.

Properly observing The Lord's Supper in the Church always includes an odd mixture of the somber and the celebratory. The bread and the cup point to the sacrifice of the Son, but they also symbolize the substitution of His death on behalf of the sinner. The Lord's Supper releases a bittersweet memory, but it is a reminder that the blood of Jesus was poured out, not as "mere symbolism," but rather as an offer of life-changing salvation. When celebrating The Lord's Supper it is important to never forget the nails. On the other hand, The Lord's Supper should never end without a reminder of the importance of the key—identification with the sacrifice of Jesus.

Identification with the sacrifice of Jesus begins with thanking Him for His death upon the Cross, personally. But knowing Jesus poured out His blood is not the same thing as identifying with His death. It was both public and personal when the Jewish fathers identified with the death of the animal they brought to the temple. Their identification with the consequences of their sin required scandalous public shame and a sense of personal loss.

Grace is free, but it has never come cheap. Forgiveness for sin always comes at a price. Like the old song says, *Jesus Paid it All.* Thank You, Jesus.

..................................

**NOTE TO SELF:** The sacrifice of the blood of Jesus cost Him His life. For you to be born again by His death, you must be identified with His sacrifice, not just be notified about it. Having an education about the sacrifice of Jesus does not lead to universal salvation. Identification with the sacrifice of Jesus is the key to personal salvation.

# 34

# THE BREAD

..............................

*For I pass on to you what I received from the Lord himself.*
*On the night when he was betrayed, the Lord Jesus took*
*some bread and gave thanks to God for it. Then he broke it*
*in pieces and said, "This is My body, which is given for you.*
*Do this to remember me"* (1 Corinthians 11:23–24 NLT).

"Yuck!" That was my first thought after I bit down on one of
the little square pellets that had been passed out in our church
during the ordinance of The Lord's Supper. After the morning
service, I made my way to the front of the church, where the
glasses of juice and bread were covered by a white, starched
tablecloth. While the adults were milling around and giving
each other the right hand of Christian fellowship, I snuck my
hand under the tablecloth and grabbed one of the forbidden
pellets, and popped it into my mouth. It was terrible. I was so
disappointed. Yeast-free bread didn't make much sense to me
as a four-year-old. My perspective on it has changed quite a bit
in the last 60 years. Thank God it has.

The bread of the Passover was prepared without the use of

yeast. This same kind of flatbread was the specific choice and held prophetic significance when *the Lord Jesus took some bread and gave thanks to God for it* (vs. 23).

Preparation for the bread had taken place on a night in Egypt, hundreds of years before the Cross when enslaved Hebrews were told by Moses to prepare a meal, which included bread baked without yeast. He further instructed them to take the life of a lamb and place its blood on the doorposts of their home. It was on that night God sent His death angel to pass over the homes of the obedient, but to take the firstborn of all those who did not prepare and partake of the Passover meal (see Exodus 11).

Paul corrected the early Church for misusing and abusing The Lord's Supper by turning it into an expression of exclusion, extravagance, and excess. He returned them to the basics, once again, utilizing bread that had little taste, but held powerful meaning with its absence of yeast.

*Jesus took some bread and gave thanks to God for it* (vs. 23). Jesus elevated the past meaning of the bread when He identified it with its new purpose. Then He thanked the Father for it.

The Lord Jesus was, and remains, the beloved Son of the Father. The Father loved Him before the foundation of the world, and loved Him no less when He gave His Son to die on the Cross for the world.

*For God so loved the world, that he gave his only begotten Son, that whosoever believeth in him should not perish, but have everlasting life* (John 3:16 KJV).

The Passover lamb selected as a proper sacrifice for this feast was a unique animal. It was the firstborn, without blemish, or mark. It was not enough for the blood of an animal to be shed—it must have been the best that could have been offered, and therefore, given with a sense of loss. Sin exacts a high price.

Jesus identified the bread that contained no yeast with His own sinless life. The rabbis compared sin and yeast as powerful agents of influence. Neither of them was easily hidden from view when they had completed their work.

..............................

**NOTE TO SELF:** Jesus thanked God He had nothing to hide from His Father or from His followers. When He prayed, He offered Himself sinless and blameless for your sin. Thank You, Jesus. Observing The Lord's Supper, at the very least, should be an expression of prayerful gratitude to the Father for the gift of His Son.

## TALK LESS! PRAY MORE!

# 35

# THE GARDEN

..............................

*"Sit here while I go over there to pray."*
—Jesus (Matthew 26:36 NLT)

One of my favorite memories on our last trip to Israel was walking with my wife, Dana, in the Garden of Gethsemane, and claiming one of the giant olive trees as our own. This special place of prayer symbolized for us the answered prayers we had received from the Father during her six-year battle with breast cancer. The Garden is filled with these great, ancient trees, and one of them bears our prayers of gratitude for answered prayer. This place holds great symbolic and substantive significance to us. We have felt Jesus pray for us through the darkest hours of our lives. There is nothing like it.

Following The Lord's Supper, Jesus invited three of His disciples to accompany Him to the olive grove, known as Gethsemane, located a short distance from the Old City (Jerusalem). Apparently, Jesus didn't expect too much out of His disciples in the area of prayer that night. (Unfortunately, too many contemporary disciples are still sitting, while Jesus is praying. But I digress.)

Jesus was *anguished and distressed*—He revealed to Peter, James, and John: *"My soul is crushed with grief to the point of death. Stay here and keep watch with me"* (Matthew 26:37–38 NLT).

In Scripture, great doors swing open on small hinges. Within the space of one hour, in a secluded olive grove on a hillside overlooking the city of Jerusalem, Jesus prayed out His grieving soul to His Father the most pivotal prayer in human history:

> *"My Father! If it is possible, let this cup of suffering*
> *be taken away from me. Yet I want your will*
> *to be done, not mine"* (vs. 39 NLT).

Through prayer, the Son faced His Father with complete honesty. Honest to God prayer led the Son to the point of absolute obedience to the Father.

To everyone else, the garden looked like a gardenia in a garbage can. Looks can be deceiving. This quiet secluded spot in the middle of the chaos and confusion of the crowded streets of a busy city was actually a battlefield. The battle that took place that night in the garden was not between good and evil. It was between "Mine" and "Thine"—honest to God prayer always is. The temptation to confuse a good idea with God's idea—or "My Will" with "Thy Will." Jesus gave some great advice to His disciples that night in Matthew 26:

> *"Keep watch and pray, so that you will not*
> *give in to temptation"* (vs. 41 NLT).

For over 2,000 years, those who have followed in the footsteps of the prayerless disciples have been led into temptation. By sleeping through "the battle of the wills," they fail to apply the same wise counsel of the Son.

Prayerlessness leads to weakness in the face of temptation. This only happens . . . EVERY TIME.

> *"Go ahead and sleep. Have your rest.*
> *But look—the time has come"* (vs. 45 NLT).

There came a point in the garden when Jesus allowed His disciples to live with their own choices and face the consequences of their own decisions. By sleeping, they sought their own version of rest and missed out on His. Those who are tireless in the pursuit of their own will ignore His wisdom and miss out on the Son's rest.

> *"Come to Me, all who are weary and heavy-laden, and I*
> *will give you rest. Take My yoke upon you and learn from*
> *Me, for I am gentle and humble in heart, And YOU WILL*
> *FIND REST FOR YOUR SOULS"* (Matthew 11:28–29).

"Come . . . and Rest" is a sign in Tempe, Arizona. These huge letters hang over the entrance of a church as an invitation to all who enter. Sitting in the gridlocked traffic in the withering heat of an Arizona summer, the letters have a mirage-like, shimmering appearance. Weary souls with white-knuckled grips on their steering wheels and sweat-filled eyes can see the sign from the street, like an oasis in the desert. The kind of rest Jesus offers still refreshes the weariest of souls and is only a prayer away. "Come . . . and Rest!"

Believing prayer is the process of a child learning to transfer the ownership of a personal problem into the hands of the Father in the name of His Son. Prayer warriors learn to release their grip on their own will and worries.

Prayerlessness creates prayer worriers who want their own way and their own rest. They tighten their grip on their personal problems until their worries become valued, private possessions that give them no rest.

Believing prayer finds R.E.S.T. by Releasing Every Single Thing.

...............................

**NOTE TO SELF:** The disciples watched and slept while Jesus watched and prayed. Your rest and the Son's rest are two very different things. Rest taken at the expense of prayer always leads to weakness in the face of temptation. Rest received in the yoke leads to fresh strength to overcome. When you come to Jesus in believing prayer, you will find His R.E.S.T. by Releasing Every Single Thing. Follow Jesus.

## TALK LESS! PRAY MORE!

# 36

# THE HOUR

..............................

*"Sit here until I have prayed"* (Mark 14:32).

When I was 20 years old, I stayed up all night driving from Waco, Texas to New York City by myself. I was trying to outrun a snowstorm and get home for Christmas. The storm rolled up the eastern seaboard, and chased me through the Shenandoah Valley all the way to Long Island. By the time I had been behind the steering wheel for 28 hours, I was suffering from terminal white line fever, and the loss of depth perception from snowflakes flying into my high beams. It is not something I recommend, but is not impossible.

I can remember at that same age, praying for one hour seemed like a lifetime to me. When your "want to" and "can do" team up, there is not much that can stand in the way. The disciples had very little of either one.

This may be one of the most unusual statements of Jesus recorded by Mark in his brief Gospel account. Peter, James, and John, the men who heard these words, really took them to heart. They sat down, and then proceeded to fall asleep as Jesus poured His heart out to the Father. It was not their finest hour.

These three disciples, often referred to as the inner circle of Jesus, must have left their chalk at home. They drew no prayer circle around themselves. Instead, they pulled their warm cloaks around their shoulders and fell asleep. When Jesus found them sleeping, He said, *"Could you not keep watch for one hour?"* (vs. 37).

Peter, James, and John were not new disciples, but rather seasoned followers of Jesus. Sometimes those who have followed Jesus the longest begin to believe they have the least to learn from Him.

By their response, these three disciples have become a prototype, or the patron saints, of the prayerless contemporary church. While Jesus interceded for His followers and pleaded with the Father, His closest followers sat and slept through the battle. It must have been hard for Jesus to watch. It still is.

In all fairness to these three disciples, it is difficult to stay awake after a long day and a good meal. But still, hearing their closest friend cry out in anguish for over an hour should have caused enough discomfort to keep them awake. Anyone with any sort of love for a hurting friend will sit up with them until their cries come to an end or the crisis has passed. The disciples didn't. They sat, they slept, and they missed out on what God was doing.

Prayerless disciples always will.

Jesus invited His closest disciples to a front row seat to the greatest battle of His life. It was not a battle between life and death. Many men had died on a cross, and Jesus wouldn't be the first or the last. Syrian Christians have taught the Church that the cross is still a real instrument of death.

The invitation of Jesus to come with Him to the garden was a once in a lifetime opportunity to see and hear Him battle with

His own will, and watch it die to God's will for His life. He told His disciples to sit. He did not tell them to sleep. Sitting led to sleeping, and they missed out on the significance of the hour.

Before his death, Ron Dunn wrote a powerful book on prayer, *Don't Just Stand There, Pray Something*. It was a call for people to turn the slightest circumstance or the greatest crisis into an opportunity to pray and see God at work in both. Thanks, Ron. You are missed.

Too often, even the closest disciple can panic in the face of an insane crisis or miss the significance of a mundane circumstance. Those who believe in a Sovereign God and sing of His amazing grace should be the first to remember that life is not a series of haphazard accidents—it is filled with divine appointments disguised as unnecessary interruptions.

The School of Prayer is open every hour, on the hour, and class is always in session. The curriculum is not a discernment of some secret code of disconnected unlucky dots and lucky dashes. Advancement in the School of Prayer is based on clear, unbroken communication with the Spirit of the risen Lord, and immediate obedience to the Word of God.

Those who enroll in the School of Prayer don't sleep in class—they race to the front row to be as close as they can to the Teacher. They maintain prayerful, consistent companionship with Jesus until the lesson has been learned.

When these three sleepy disciples were invited by Jesus to sit on the front row of the class He was holding in the garden, it was not a reward for their advancement but a statement on their weakness. Facing temptation in a state of prayerlessness always feeds weakness.

The rest of the jealous disciples must have resented not being invited to the garden. They had been arguing about which one of them held the highest status and deserved the greatest position. It must have appeared to them that Jesus had invited the teacher's pets to go on a field trip, but they didn't realize Peter, James, and John were being held after class for further study, and were about to fail an unexpected pop quiz.

...........................

**NOTE TO SELF:** Every time you think you are advancing in The School of Prayer, you need to prepare yourself for a lesson you are about to learn. The School of Prayer is filled with pop quizzes that will deflate your balloon of spiritual pride. There is always someone who has learned more than you, and you have a great deal yet to learn. Sit at the feet of Jesus and stay awake. You don't want to stay after school.

## TALK LESS! PRAY MORE!

# 37

# THE CUSTOM

..............................

*And He came out and proceeded as was His custom to the Mount of Olives; and the disciples also followed Him. When He arrived at the place, He said to them, "Pray that you may not enter into temptation." And He withdrew from them about a stone's throw, and He knelt down and began to pray, saying, "Father, if You are willing, remove this cup from Me; yet not My will, but Yours be done"* (Luke 22:39–42).

My Aunt Isabelle lived across the road from an elderly, slightly built farmer named Levi. He had two huge Clydesdale horses he often harnessed to plow his Pennsylvania farmland. I loved making my way to Levi's barn to watch him handle his team. When Levi walked into the barn, he would reach for their harnesses. Both horses would start snorting and pawing at the ground with their great hooves. Levi would then open the gate to their stalls, and they would follow him out. Each would stand in front of him and lower their heads to allow him to place their collar and harnesses on them. Each one yielded their will to the will of their master. Together they did great things, guided by his will.

Jesus prayed and obeyed. Follow His lead, away from the temptation to desire for your will be done. Yield to the Father's will for your life.

**THE PATTERN:** Jesus set a pattern of prayer which He frequently modeled for His disciples. His custom of prayer was not easily reproduced, but was readily recognized by them. They saw Him pray, heard Him pray, and they even came to Him and said, *"Lord, teach us to pray"* (Luke 11:1). They didn't realize the Son's pattern for prayer was sustained by His passion for the Father. His disciples could follow His pattern for prayer, but would never experience the power of prayer until they shared His passion for the Father.

**THE PLACE:** The Mount of Olives was a quiet place separated from the crowded streets, chaos, and confusion of the Old City of Jerusalem.

Situated on a hillside overlooking the Eastern Gate, Jesus would often withdraw to this special place to get alone with God. Those who have discovered the place of prayer know the value of it. Those who have not found their place of prayer must find it and race to it, early and often.

**THE PREVENTION:** One of the main reasons Jesus gave His disciples for maintaining a disciplined life of prayer was to develop their capacity to resist temptation. Prayer and the Word of God were the one-two punch Jesus used to defeat the temptations of the evil one. Wise disciples follow His lead, and in their weakness, find fresh strength. Fools rush in where angels fear to tread and fall for every lie of the evil one.

**THE PURPOSE:** Jesus prayed for His will to be conformed to the will of the Father. Perhaps nothing expresses the purpose of prayer more than the simple phrase: *yet not My will, but Yours* (Luke 22:42). The unction of prayer is found between the junction of "yet" and "but." Believing prayer is where "Mine" is transformed to "Thine."

The difference between a prayer warrior and a prayer poser hinges on the little word, "yet." Posers are always willing to pray for the Father's blessing on their lives as long as they don't have to yield to the Father's direction of their lives. Praying and yielding should be synonyms. They are not always the same thing, but prayer warriors should make sure they are.

A prayer warrior prays long enough to bring their will into line with the will of the Father just as Jesus did. His followers must take their stand with Him by kneeling and yielding to the Father's will for their lives.

*Delayed obedience is still disobedience.* —Henry Blackaby

Seven years ago I was having dinner with my father, when he asked me if God had clarified His direction for my life. I responded that I was convinced God wanted me to launch a new prayer ministry for the local Church. He asked, "Have you resigned your position as pastor?" I said, "No. I am trying to arrange things for a smooth transition." He said, "If God has told you to do something, you might want to think about being obedient."

Those words hit me like a ton of bricks. At 60 years of age, I suddenly felt like a rebellious teenager trying to negotiate a better deal after breaking curfew. I knew what I had to do. I prayed and obeyed, and six years later, God has proven Himself faithful to us, and *TALK LESS! PRAY MORE! Ministries* is moving forward, preparing pastors of the local Church to lead their people to pray and prepare for the next Great Awakening. The best is yet to come.

...............................

**NOTE TO SELF:** Have you prayed enough, yet? As long as you are debating God's will, you are not obeying His will. Praying and yielding are two sides of the same coin of prayer. Offering the Father your prayers without yielding to His will with immediate obedience is nothing but counterfeit Christianity.

### TALK LESS! PRAY MORE!

# WHEN A TRAIN GOES THROUGH A TUNNEL AND IT GETS DARK, YOU DON'T THROW AWAY THE TICKET AND JUMP OFF. YOU SIT STILL AND TRUST THE ENGINEER.

## CORRIE TEN BOOM

# 38

# THE UNFORGIVEN

..............................

*"Father, forgive them; for they do not*
*know what they are doing"* (Luke 23:34).

Forgiving one man for what he did to my family took longer than I ever expected it would. I am not proud to say, but for 15 years it required me to offer forgiveness to him more often than I wanted to do it. One morning, before dawn, waiting for the driver to shuttle me to the Boston airport, a voice from the back row of the van called my name. It was a friend who was familiar with what I had experienced at the hands of the man I had forgiven. He informed me of the man's recent death—it had been prolonged and painful. I expressed my sincere regret at hearing it. I was not surprised by my words, but by the spirit with which they came from my heart.

After years of praying and forgiving him, I discovered in that moment that forgiveness had finally reached my heart. It was a revelation of how the Spirit of Christ works to bring about an answer to the same kind of prayer Jesus prayed. Forgiveness did not come like a hammer to nail down my rights, and make me whole. It came quietly, like the dew. It arrived unannounced and unheard, but with effective enough power to soften my heart in the process. Praying involves staying in the furnace of forgiveness, until letting go of your rights. Trust the Father to make things right on Earth and in Heaven. It is His call to make.

Nothing expresses the prayer life of Jesus more succinctly and accurately than in Luke 23:34. Within the space of a dozen words, Jesus called out to the Father, not for vengeance upon His executioners, but for the forgiveness of them. What a Savior.

In the constitution of the Kingdom outlined in The Sermon on the Mount, Jesus said to His followers, *"Pray for those who persecute you"* (Matthew 5:44). This statement is amazing, but it should not be surprising. However, it is easier to say it than to pray it. Can I get a witness?

To forgive someone is to let go of an offense immediately rather than hold onto it for eternity. Those who have difficulty with the concept of forgiveness are often held up on the injustice of letting someone get away with something they did wrong. Letting go of an offense is not the same thing as letting someone get away with it. It's the transferring of the offense and the offender over to another Judge's jurisdiction.

Forgiveness is so much more than just letting go. Jesus prayed to the Father and interceded for the forgiveness of His offenders. He pleaded for them and left them in His Father's hands. Then He went to the Cross and died for them. His intercession for His enemies led to His crucifixion. Letting go of His case against His executioners led Jesus to take up His Cross on their behalf. His followers should do the same for their enemies.

Forgiveness involves letting go of the offense by interceding for the offender. Praying for those who have wronged us is more than a pious devotional exercise—it involves developing a well-worn path to the Cross and a daily dying to one's own personal rights and preferences.

Forgiveness is a powerful concept but it does not become a life-changing experience until it has been delivered to those who need it the most.

Conceiving the idea of forgiveness is a poor substitute for placing it as a gift in the hands of an enemy. Jesus did not expect forgiveness to be delivered from the hands and hearts of prayerless disciples. The unforgiven need forgiveness the most, but will never receive it from the prayerless.

Expecting forgiveness to be delivered from prayerless people is like expecting sweet fruit from a rootless tree. The fruit of forgiveness doesn't fall far from the root of the tree grounded in love.

> *"You have heard that is was said, 'YOU SHALL*
> *LOVE YOUR NEIGHBOR and hate your enemy.'*
> *But I say to you, love your enemies and pray for*
> *those who persecute you"* (Matthew 5:43–44).

Jesus taught differently than the respected rabbis of His day. They fell back on the oral tradition that was grounded in The Law. Jesus played against their tendency to trust tradition and miss the truth by stating over and over again to the people, *"You have heard . . . But I say to you."* There was a new sheriff in town, and Jesus was not only going to uphold The Law, He was going to fulfill it.

Jesus prayed during the chaos and confusion of the crucifixion, *"Father, forgive them; for they do not know what they are doing"* (vs. 34). His powerful words pouring out from His hurting heart to the Father on behalf of those intent upon hurting

Him remain the industry standard for Christian compassion today. Thank You, Jesus.

English jurisprudence holds, "Ignorance of the law is no defense." Jesus did not excuse or explain away the ignorance of those who were intent on killing Him. He interceded for His killers in spite of their ignorance. Jesus didn't use their ignorance as a fine point of His case against them in the court of law. He prayed for His killers in the Father's court of love, let them go, left their fate in His Father's hands, and then gave His life to take their place on the Cross for their sins.

Praying for those who persecute you identifies you with the Cross and the prayer life of Jesus. Prayer conformed the will of Jesus to the will of the Father. His followers must not settle for anything less and can offer their enemies nothing more.

Don't panic in the face of persecution—pray for people who are the source when you are the recipient of it. Praying for your enemies in the name of Jesus will see you through it and develop you into a conduit for the Father's love to the unforgiven.

..............................

**NOTE TO SELF:** Being called upon to pray for people who have done their best to do their worst to you holds a not so hidden warning for you. People who need to be forgiven by you have wronged you. You are not mistaken. You are not being judgmental or paranoid. There are people in the world who have hurt you and they will hurt you again. But pray for them anyway.

When you let go of the offense, they are not getting away with it—you have just transferred their case to another court. Pray for your enemies to fall into the hands of the Father. Dying to self keeps you from taking it on yourself to punish your enemies for what they have done to you. When you let go of the offense, your enemies are not getting away with anything. You are leaving them in the Father's hands to receive His direction and correction.

**TALK LESS! PRAY MORE!**

## Two things break God's heart: Rebellion and Repentance.

DON MILLER

# 39

# THE OPENING

..............................

*He took the bread and blessed it, and breaking*
*it, He began giving it to them. Then their eyes*
*were opened and they recognized Him; and He*
*vanished from their sight* (Luke 24:30–31).

One of the lessons Dana and I learned in her fight against breast cancer was the need to stop talking about the crisis we were facing, and to start praying about it. The more hot air we blew into the unwanted crisis, the more we kept expanding it like a big, ugly balloon. Filled with our fear, the balloon got in our faces, and kept blocking out the presence of Jesus. He was there all along, but we just couldn't see Him. The more we focused on the crisis, the more it took our eyes off of Him. The couple on the Road to Emmaus was in a similar crisis. It wasn't until they shared a prayer with Jesus that they really saw Him face-to-face.

When Jesus found them, they were on a downhill path, both figuratively and literally. He found them discouraged, disheartened, and engaged in an intense discussion of all the events that had taken place in the city of Jerusalem. They had a lot to talk about, but as they descended down the road out of town, they couldn't make sense out of any of it. Jesus looked for the right opening and invited Himself into their private conversation.

*While they were talking and discussing, Jesus Himself approached and began traveling with them* (Luke 24:15).

Prayer is the only option available to people who are looking for the Father's direction, protection, and correction. Talking through any insane crisis and every mundane circumstance is not intercession. It is procrastination, a failed attempt to frame the debate and make sense out of the senseless.

Talking something to death is a fool's errand—it sheds more heat than light on the crisis of the hour and breathes new life into the mundane circumstances that kill, steal, and destroy joy. The enemy invites people to talk until their brains fall out, but Jesus invites the brokenhearted to pour out their prayers to Him. Big difference.

When Jesus approached the couple on the road they were in need of insight. Looking into their own minds and hearts for answers that only the Father could give and the Son could explain, was not going to end well for either one of them.

Jesus approached them while they were stumbling over each other through the darkest moment of their lives and offered His presence. Thank God Jesus still does.

*"What are these words that you are exchanging with one another?"* (Luke 24:17).

With this abrupt interruption, Jesus scheduled a divine appointment with two people who needed to hear from Him, more than they needed to say something to one another. Perhaps this is the opening the Father is looking for in the lives of the contemporary church. People coming to the end of their own rope and bringing their tangled lives to Him would be a huge improvement rather than pooling their ignorance with one another.

As these two downhearted disciples walked and talked with Jesus, their hearts were consumed in a common fire as He shared His insight with them from the Word of God. After sharing an evening meal with Jesus and hearing Him pray a blessing over the bread He shared with them, their eyes were opened. They embraced His true identity and discovered the meaning of all the "senseless" things they had experienced during the darkest hour of their lives.

*"Were not our hearts burning within us while He was . . .*
*explaining the Scriptures to us?"* (Luke 24:32).

Jesus stepped into the lives of two disciples between the breaking of His body on the Cross and the breaking of bread at an evening meal. One appeared as an insane crisis—the other was a mundane circumstance. The Father was at work in both, revealing His Son to those whose hearts were open to receive Him.

Jesus took the first available opening in an independent lecture series between two weary disciples. He asked them to stop talking to one another and to bring Him into their conversation. Their lives were never the same again. Your next prayer is the opening Jesus is looking for to make sense out of the senseless and to release His Spirit to saturate us with the next Great Awakening.

..................................

**NOTE TO SELF:** Opening your mouth to share your insight with people lost in the tall grass is a poor substitute for opening your eyes and your arms to Jesus. Don't waste any insane crisis or miss any mundane circumstance.

Pray your way through both. Either one can be an opportunity for you to invite Jesus into the chaos and the confusion. Talking postpones your divine appointment, but praying gives the Spirit the elbowroom and time to make sense out of the senseless. You talk too much and you pray too little.

## TALK LESS! PRAY MORE!

## YOUR WALK WITH GOD IS
## THE NEXT 20 SECONDS.

UNKNOWN

# 40

# THE TRANSGRESSOR

..............................

*Yet He Himself bore the sin of many,*
*And interceded for the transgressors* (Isaiah 53:12).

My friend, Vestal Blakely, stood by my side in a dingy police station in Dar es Salaam, Tanzania, and pleaded my case. He interceded for me. I stood accused of a transgression by the officer on duty. I was placed under house arrest and my Land Rover was impounded. I would not be free to leave the city until the fate of the pedestrian I had hit could be determined. If she died, I might be placed in jail. At the very least, I would be deported.

Vestal identified with me, and interceded for me. He had done nothing wrong, but if the authorities couldn't find me, they would come looking for him.

To be clear, on my best day, I am one of the transgressors and Jesus is the Intercessor. Though I have been forgiven, I am capable of crossing over to the dark side and breaking fellowship with Jesus, the Light. Praying does not make me perfect, but it shines His Light on my sin, and He puts me back on the path to the Father's forgiveness.

As the Intercessor—Jesus lives to bring people to the Father. His death on the Cross expressed His intercessory mission on Earth. Seated at the right hand of the Father He continues His ministry of intercession in Heaven to both save and strengthen believers.

> *Christ Jesus is He who died, yes, rather who*
> *was raised, who is at the right hand of God,*
> *who also intercedes for us* (Romans 8:34).

Jesus, the risen Christ, lives to make intercession for those who draw near to God in His name. Prayer opens the door to an audience with the Father. The prayerful are childlike, seeking His direction, protection, and correction, early and often. The prayerless are childish and rebellious, hiding from the face of the Father fearing His assessment of their behavior. They rob themselves of both the privilege of His presence and the joy of His forgiveness.

> *But Jesus, on the other hand, because He continues*
> *forever, holds His priesthood permanently. Therefore*
> *He is able also to save forever those who draw near*
> *to God through Him, since He always lives to make*
> *intercession for them* (Hebrews 7:24–25).

Jesus prayed to the Father through every tear, trial, and triumph. He refused to allow anything or anyone to turn Him into a rebellious child or rob Him of the privilege of coming into the Father's presence. Jesus prayed and obeyed—as His followers we should do no less.

Prayerlessness is the spirit of independence released from the heart of a rebel. Prayerfulness is the spirit of repentance and expresses the spirit of dependence. The obedient child of the Father prays and obeys.

Jesus lives to make it possible for His followers to draw near to the Father as obedient children. The followers of Jesus Christ should not be surprised that the path to the Father is paved with the same stones and stumbling blocks Jesus encountered.

Ordinary and extraordinary obstacles have a way of getting in the face of the prayerful. Obedient prayer warriors follow the Intercessor's lead and allow His Spirit to guide them to the face of the Father, even when they fall on their faces.

Perhaps one of the most powerful statements about the life of Jesus found in Scripture is, *He learned obedience from the things which He suffered* (Hebrews 5:8). Jesus learned to bring His tears, trials, and triumphs to the Father. His death on the Cross was not a result of unanswered prayers—it was both intercession and an answer to His prayers.

Prayer warriors should expect to encounter the same kind of learning curve that Jesus faced when enrolled in The School of Prayer. Prayer is learned behavior. Those who rebel against the lessons of prayer will find they have to stay after school, until they have learned them.

*In the days of His flesh, He offered up both prayers and supplications with loud crying and tears to the One able to save Him from death, and He was heard because of His piety. Although He was a Son,* **He learned obedience from the things which He suffered** *(Hebrews 5:7–8 emphasis added).*

There is simply no substitute for personal, prolonged, persistent, private, personal prayer. Jesus did it while He ministered on Earth. He continues His unique ministry of intercession in

Heaven. Prayerlessness is an expression of rebellion, but prayerfulness is an expression of repentance. Both break the heart of the Father. Wise children pray and obey the will of the Father.

..............................

**NOTE TO SELF:** Prayerless rebellion generated by the tears and trials of life will leave you vulnerable to an attack of the enemy. Take every tear and trial to Jesus immediately. Let Him make sense out of it. Prayerlessness can also be generated after a triumph. Celebrate every victory, but prayerlessness will make you a victim of victory. Prayerfully place every triumph in the hands of Jesus and avoid the slightest prideful, prayerless detour from the Father's presence. Jesus invited His first disciples with the words, "Follow Me." Jesus, the Intercessor, still does. Through every tear, every trial, and every triumph.

### TALK LESS! PRAY MORE!

EPILOGUE

# THE NEXT GREAT AWAKENING

..............................

Perhaps the most revolutionary thing about Jesus was His prayer life. He was constantly turning His face to the Father, turning His followers around, and urging them to show Him respect. He desired His followers to pray with the same kind of passion and sense of direction He had.

> *In the days of His flesh, He offered up both prayers and supplications with loud crying and tears to the One able to save Him from death, and He was heard because of His piety* (Hebrews 5:7).

I remember the Jesus Revolution of the late 60s and early 70s. It was messy, disorderly, disruptive, and I totally miss it. During those crazy days, it was popular to refer to Jesus as a revolutionary. The confusion and chaos of the counter-culture movement was sweeping the nation, and it seemed hip for uncool Christians seeking to sound relevant to buy into the lingo.

These early hipsters seemed to think of Jesus as some kind of socially evolved, safe, and sanctified Che Guevara, minus the beret.

**THE PRAYERS:** Jesus offered His prayers to the Father out of respect for Him and deference to Him. The Son gave honor where honor was due. At the very heart of prayer is a reverence and respect for the Father.

Prayerless, rebellious children have no respect for the Father, so they don't offer Him prayer. Before prayerlessness can be turned into prayerfulness, it must be called by its right name, and recognized for what it is. It is a lack of respect for the Father and rebellion from His direction, protection, and correction.

Jesus was no rebel. He was a revolutionary in the sense that He turned people around. His life revolved around prayer to the Father. His followers should turn their faces to the Father in prayer, in the name of the Son.

Prayerlessness is a sign of rebellion and disrespect to the Father.

**THE SUPPLICATIONS:** Believing prayer is heard and answered. The essence of supplication is the supplying of what is needed to meet an expressed need. When Jesus made supplications to the Father, He expected to be heard and supplied. As His followers, we should expect no less. When you pray in His name, and yield to the will of the Father, your prayers will be filled with expectancy.

**THE CRYING:** Prayer expressed by loud crying is an explosion of passion which cannot be contained in a whispered request. Jesus prayed knowing the Father heard him—without worrying if He was being overheard. Children cry until a parent responds to their need, and sometimes they keep crying even after their need has been met. Crying out to the Father was not unusual for Jesus. It should be a birthmark on those who follow Him.

**THE TEARS:** Jesus prayed with tears flowing from His eyes, not just with requests pouring out of His mouth. His prayers were in touch with His heart, and His heart longed for a touch from the Father.

**THE ONE:** The Father was the One who could save the Son from death. Death by crucifixion was an execution, designed to be painful, and last a long time. It was cruel and unusual, but it was not punishment used to teach the victim a lesson. It was not an education—it was annihilation.

But the Son did not fear death by crucifixion. He abhorred the thought of the Cross as separation. In that moment, the Father turned His face from the Son. Death on the Cross meant the end of a relationship between the Father and the Son that had never been broken. Sin would break it. Only the Father could heal it and make it whole again. Jesus prayed with passion for it.

**THE HEARING:** The Father hears the prayers of Jesus. His prayers of intercession go directly to the One who is able to save. The prayers of Jesus go directly to the source of strength and salvation, the Father.

Believing prayer is not wishing for something to be true, and wondering if it is. Believing prayer gains a hearing in the presence of the Father, in the name of the Son. Believing prayer not only seeks to have a hearing in the presence of the Father, through the Son—it waits and listens to the voice of the Spirit for an answer, no matter how long it takes, or whatever it may be.

**THE PIETY:** Jesus is heard because He is right in the eyes of the Father. The piety of the Son is expressed by His reverence and obedience to the will of the Father. Piety describes the character and the conduct of a person who has a respect and reverence for God.

Rather than rushing in where angels fear to tread, Jesus always got His marching orders from His Father. Fools rush in, but Jesus was no fool. His cautious and circumspect behavior, expressed by respectful prayer, was not a result of His fear of man, but His fear of God.

Prayerless people may appear fearless, but they are foolish children racing ahead of the Father. Breathing in their own ether, and reading their own press clippings, may make a name for themselves, but it will often bring shame upon the name of the Father.

...............................

**NOTE TO SELF:** Start your own revolution. Turn around and face the Father. Stop running from Him and start praying to Him, in the name of Jesus.

Anything less is rebellion. No matter how busy you are, or how successful your prayerless efforts are in the eyes of others, your best efforts are nothing but rebellion in the eyes of the Father. You are not pious because you are perfect, but because you know your own limitations. Come to the One, the Father, in the name of the Son, to receive His Spirit's direction, protection, and correction for your life.

And always remember . . .

## TALK LESS! PRAY MORE!

# ABOUT THE AUTHOR

........................

Dr. Gary Miller is married to Dana and is the father of two grown children, Ashley, married to Brent Warren, and Allyson. After graduating from Baylor University and Southwestern Baptist Theological Seminary, Dr. Miller served as a Southern Baptist pastor for four decades in Texas, Arizona, Georgia, and Oklahoma. The Millers now reside in Fort Worth, Texas and conduct TALK LESS! PRAY MORE! Conferences. They equip pastors to utilize personal and corporate prayer to develop healthy churches and homes, and to pray for the next Great Awakening.

**CONTACT THE AUTHOR:**

PO Box 96165
Southlake, TX 76092

**BOOKING INFORMATION:**

garydonmiller.com
gmillerlight@gmail.com
817-975-5054

**FOLLOW US:**

/TalkLessPrayMore
@garydonmiller
/talklesspraymore

#talklesspraymore

TALK LESS! PRAY MORE!

66386192R00106

Made in the USA
Lexington, KY
13 August 2017